Further Zen Conversations

On the scope, practice, and future of North American Zen

Richard Bryan McDaniel

For Lauren,
welcome to the family

FURTHER ZEN CONVERSATIONS
On the scope, practice, and future of North American Zen
Richard Bryan McDaniel

Text © Richard Bryan McDaniel, 2023
Cover graphic: NataLima, Shutterstock
Author photo: Joan McDaniel
All rights reserved

ISBN 978-1-896559-94-0

Book design: John Negru

Published by
The Sumeru Press Inc.
PO Box 75, Manotick Main Post Office,
Manotick, ON, Canada K4M 1A2

LIBRARY AND ARCHIVES CANADA CATALOGUING IN PUBLICATION

Title: Further Zen conversations : on the scope, practice, and future of North American Zen / Richard Bryan McDaniel.
Names: McDaniel, Richard Bryan, author.
Description: Includes index.
Identifiers: Canadiana 20230158153 | ISBN 9781896559940 (softcover)
Subjects: LCSH: Zen Buddhists—Canada—Interviews. | LCSH: Zen Buddhists—United States—Interviews. | LCSH: Zen priests—Canada—Interviews. | LCSH: Zen priests—United States Interviews. | LCSH: Zen Buddhism—Canada. | LCSH: Zen Buddhism—United States. | LCGFT: Interviews.
Classification: LCC BQ9298 .M342 2023 | DDC 294.3/927092271 dc23

 For more information about The Sumeru Press visit us at *www.sumeru-books.com*

Table of Contents

Foreword
7

Preface
9

1 Varieties of Zen Experience
13

2 Is Zen Unique?
43

3 What Do Zen Teachers Teach?
55

4 Zen and Psychology
75

5 The Impact of Zen Practice
91

6 Vows and Precepts
109

7 Looking Forward
127

Epilogue: Online
151

Appendices

1 The Precepts 161
2 The Bodhisattva Vows 167
3 Affirming Faith in Mind 169
4 Torei Enji's Bodhisattva's Vow 175
Index of Interviews 177
Glossary 179

Foreword
Rafe Jnan Martin

Rick McDaniel's two-book set, *Zen Conversations* and *Further Zen Conversations*, goes to the horse's mouth – Zen teachers themselves – to open up the evolving tale of North American Zen.

Most of the contemporary teachers interviewed are homegrown, having trained in the US or Canada, not in Japan. Many did so with first and second generation Western, not Asian, teachers. Plus, as they are spread across a number of active lineages, these thematically organized conversations offer readers an expansive view.

How Rick, a long-time Zen practitioner, came to travel around North America in-person and, later, after COVID, by Skype and Zoom to chat with contemporary teachers is a tale in itself, one that gets told via the Prefaces of the two books. Yet once he gets these conversations going, he rarely intrudes further but simply allows each teacher or senior student to speak for themselves.

Because of Rick's earlier series of books on the teacher-by-teacher transmission of Zen from China to Japan and then on through the recent North American generations, his *Zen Conversations* and *Further Zen Conversations* rest on a solid foundation, and the questions he asks are wide ranging: Where is North American Zen teaching and practice at these days? How's it doing? What are the challenges and issues? How does it deal with tradition and innovation, with the balance of personal and communal practice, with monastic and lay styles and forms, with the demands of citizenship – i.e., environmental awareness and action and politics – while at the same time not watering down actual, intimate, ongoing *practice*? And what about psychology? In short, how'd we get to where we are and what might the future (or possible futures) of North American Zen look like? In fact, is there even such a thing as "a North American Zen" or are there many, each with its own views and responses?

Rick organizes the conversations he's gathered thematically rather than teacher by teacher. And it works. And, yet ... it's such a rich meal it's almost like a buffet of desserts – pies, cakes, petit fours – piled high. Reading too much at one time can lead to a sugar high or a bit of a tummy ache. So, even though some of my own conversations with Rick are included in *Further Zen Conversations*, my recommendation is to go slow, read a section or so, then, stop and digest. Adding some leavening between such "reads" might be wise, too. Which might mean dipping into the Zen writings of such gifted ancestors as Hakuin, Dogen, or Ryokan. Or facing the work of actual practice as presented in Philip Kapleau's *The Three Pillars of Zen* or Robert Aitken's *Taking the Path of Zen* or in Aitken or Shibyama's books on the *Gateless Barrier* (*Wumen kuan*; *Mumonkan*). Or just sitting and facing a wall, letting everything go, discovering how little we know, how little can be known, and, indeed, known by whom? Such little bits of bitterness will help the sweet medicine go down. You won't simply be coasting in on someone else's words.

Regardless, Rick has graciously done all the necessary legwork. Or, to turn to a food-related old Zen metaphor: he's kindly peeled the lychee for us and put it in our mouths. All we have to do now is chew. (By the way, *Zen Conversations*' introduction offers a history of North American Zen.) To be clear – for one person to report on the state of North American Zen, allowing teachers of diverse styles and lineages to speak for themselves is rather remarkable, revealing deep faith in Zen's many current North American forms. (A good number of the teaching lines now active in North America are given voice here, though not all.) Admirably, Rick seems to have no personal ax to grind, and shows no need to defend what he himself might think Zen should or should not be. Of course, he selected each conversation and organized them into sections but both books show only openness toward and respect for all the various viewpoints presented. A trustworthy guide, Rick remains truly non-judgmental. Given our deeply polarized times, this is refreshing, even healing in itself. Sitting down with all sorts of Zen teachers – lay, ordained, monastic/celibate, householder; Soto, Rinzai, combined or in-between; those with large centers, those with little zendos, those with many students, those with a handful; experienced teachers and those just starting out – he puts everyone at ease and raises questions central to all.

Hats off to Rick. We are his beneficiaries and owe him a debt of gratitude. Fifty or a hundred years from now when students of religion and historians of Zen look into how what was originally an Asian religion came to flourish so naturally in North America, they will seek out these books. In them they will uncover what Zen teachers of today, themselves a living bridge between East and West, were saying, doing, and thinking. The story of the creation of an ordinary, real, genuinely North American Bodhisattvic Zen can be found in these books of simple, straightforward, thoughtful, and often heart-felt conversations.

Get the set. In the future they are bound to become heirlooms of Zen's many-roomed house.

Rafe Jnan Martin, founding teacher
Endless Path Zendo, Rochester, New York

Preface

The book I released prior to this – *Zen Conversations* – wasn't one I had intended to write.

I started writing while I was recovering from a series of only moderately successful surgeries on my left leg. My intention had been to take the Zen stories I had encountered in *teishos* (lectures), as *koans* (subjects for meditation), and in general reading and arrange them in sequential order. I had collected these stories in a series of notebooks without always understanding the relationship between the individuals described. I was also unsure why some of the people had more than one version of their name and was often caught off guard until I figured out that Zhaozhou Congshen [current Chinese usage], Chao-chou Ts'ung-shen [former Chinese usage], and Joshu Jushin [Japanese form] were the same individual.

I approached the project as a kind of jigsaw puzzle. It was something I was doing for my own sake and nothing more until my eldest daughter – herself an author – encouraged me to try to place it with a publisher. She helped me write a pitch letter which I submitted to the only company I was aware of that printed such books. I received a very polite refusal, but they added that it seemed a worthwhile project and suggested two other publishers I should consider approaching. One of these, Tuttle, proved eager enough to bring the book out that they tracked me down by phone one day.

My editor at Tuttle advised me to consider undertaking a trilogy. The working title for the book had been *The First Step East: Zen Masters of China*. The editor and the marketing people at Tuttle reversed the elements of the title, and it came out in 2012 as *Zen Masters of China: The First Step East*. It was suggested that I follow it up with a book on *Zen Masters of Japan* (Tuttle, 2013), and a third on Zen Masters of North America.

The editor also advised me to publish the book under my full name – Richard Bryan McDaniel – instead of the name I usually go by (Rick McDaniel) in order not to be confused with Pastor Rick McDaniel, a Christian evangelist and writer who, among other things, was a sometime Fox News contributor.

After changes at Tuttle's editorial offices, I was informed that they could not guarantee the third book would be released. It was my good fortune by then, however, to have been approached by John Negru of Sumeru Books who told me that if I ever decided to use a Canadian publisher, he would be pleased to be considered. He brought out the third volume of the trilogy under its original title – *The Third Step East: Zen Masters of America* – in 2015.

The Third Step East focused on the pioneers who established Zen in North America – people like Robert Aitken, Philip Kapleau, Shunryu Suzuki, Taizan Maezumi, and Walter Nowick. All but one of the individuals profiled in that book were already dead, but their immediate heirs were alive and leading communities across North America. When John and I negotiated the contract for *The Third Step*, I suggested a sequel which would look at those second-generation teachers. A small inheritance gave me the wherewithal to undertake a tour of Zen Centers throughout the continent. I began in San Francisco on March 21, 2013, and eventually conducted interviews as far east as Halifax, as far north as Montreal, and as far south as Mexico City.

The resulting manuscript – my fourth book – was published by Sumeru as *Cypress Trees in Garden: The Second Generation of Zen Teaching in North America* and was released the same year as *The Third Step*. While conducting those interviews, I became aware of and fascinated by a sub-set of authorized Zen teachers who remained practicing Roman Catholics, which resulted in a fifth book, *Catholicism and Zen* (Sumeru, 2017).

I then began work on what I intended to be my last book. In it I brought together all the material from the previous five books. I began by narrating the development of Buddhism in India, went on to describe its encounter with and modification by Daosim in China, resulting in Chan Buddhism which in turn was refined and labeled Zen in Japan, before finally taking that third step East and arriving in North America. In the final section of the book, I profiled a number of younger teachers I believed were representative of the people who would carry the tradition into the future. The book was entitled *The Story of Zen* and appeared in 2019 with a foreword by Genjo Marinello Roshi and an afterword by Dosho Port Roshi.

And that, I was fairly confident, was that. There was really nothing more for me to write about.

Then came the COVID pandemic.

When national and local governments realized the extent of the pandemic, strict measures were imposed to fight the spread of the disease. People were quarantined in their homes; businesses – and Zen Centers – closed (many never to reopen); air travel virtually came to a halt. People were told to only go out for groceries and emergencies, to avoid contact with friends and relatives, and to wear masks when they did have to be in public. It was an enormously stressful period that went on for more than a year.

My wife and I were fortunate. We live in a beautiful rural setting not far from a provincial park. We had pleasant surroundings and ample opportunity for walking and getting outside. But the fact remained that the quarantine was dreary. And so in the same way that the tedium of the repeated leg surgeries and recovery periods had led me to write *Zen Masters of China*, so the boredom of quarantine led me to review the transcripts of the more than 100 interviews I had conducted to see if there were anything in them that I could play around with to pass the time.

Rereading these interviews, I noticed how the same question posed to a dozen different authorized Zen teachers could provoke twelve very different, even divergent, responses. If one were to survey a group of Christian clerics from different regions and denominations about the basics of Christian belief, there would be a range of response but there would also be general agreement on fundamental issues. Likewise a group of Muslim clerics or Jewish religious leaders, regardless of their geographical locations, would present a generally homogenous portrait of their faith traditions. But Zen teachers, even within the same city, often presented such radically different perspectives that it was at times difficult to see how they belonged to the same admittedly broad tradition.

In *Zen Conversations*, then, I took a new approach. I focused on the range of points of view extant in North American Zen. With a minimum of commentary, I presented the reflections of 42 Zen teachers on a narrow group of topics: the function of Zen, the nature of Zen practice, the ways in which Zen had been adapted for Western practitioners, as well as their understanding of compassionate action and what has come to be known as Ecodharma. Sumeru published the book in 2021, when most Zen Centers throughout the world still had closed doors and, if they were meeting at all, were doing so through Zoom conference calls.

The book was received more warmly than I'd anticipated, and the American Zen Teachers' Association invited me to give the keynote address at their 2021 video-conferenced AGM to review some of my findings.

This current book is not a sequel to its predecessor but is a companion work. They each stand alone, although they complement one another. The 35 voices in this book are – with one major exception – deliberately different than those I depended upon in *Zen Conversations* as are the topics they reflect upon, although there are inevitable overlaps. I also include a handful of long-term practitioners and "assistant" teachers whose perspective is often different from that of people officially designated as carriers of the tradition.

I don't know if there will be any further books. I had been so certain *The Story of Zen* was going to be my final work that I dare not make any predictions. I do, however, continue to have these conversations and remain fascinated by the range of perspectives I encounter.

A note on my approach

One of the people I interviewed inquired whether I was acting as an anthropologist: "i.e., conducting fieldwork interviews from which you might choose a few anonymous quotes for the book you are writing about contemporary Zen practitioners." Or was I "working more as a journalist or documentarian."

I don't see myself as either of those. If I have a role, it is – as my granddaughter put it – as an oral historian, and as an oral historian I make an effort to be neutral. It isn't that I don't have opinions about Zen – I do, and I suspect most readers are able to discern them – but that I try not to let those opinions interfere with my description of the scope of my subject.

1
Varieties of Zen Experience

Buddhism is divided into two major streams. The older and more spartan is the Theravada, commonly practiced in Thailand, Myanmar, and Sri Lanka. The more philosophically complex, but also at times more fanciful, Mahayana, is commonly practiced in China, Japan, Vietnam, and Korea. Zen is one of several classes of the latter and is itself divided into a number of schools. It was introduced to the west in the early 20th century more as a literary phenomenon than as a religious tradition. In Europe and North America, there had been academic interest in the older – Theravada – form of Buddhism since the 19th century, but the Mahayana in general, and Zen in particular, remained largely unknown until the Japanese scholar, D.T. Suzuki, composed a series of essays in the early decades of the 20th century which won the admiration of psychologists, philosophers, artists, and even Catholic monastics.

Zen, as Suzuki presented it, was a spiritual tradition unlike the theistic religions more commonly known in the West. Belief in an external creator and divinely revealed law was replaced by a focus on human endeavour, through meditation, to attain a state variously called *satori*, awakening, or enlightenment, which alters both one's understanding of and relationship to life and the natural world. Suzuki's writings intrigued readers with tales of sages meditating for years while facing cave walls or cutting off their arms to gain access to wisdom and struggling with enigmatic koans, apparently insoluble challenges about the sound of a single hand clapping or how to demonstrate one's face before one's parents had been born. He was presenting Rinzai Zen, the type of Zen in which he had been trained. For decades, readers in the West assumed that he was representing all Zen practice. It would be the 1960s before it became generally known that there were other – often very different – varieties of Zen.[1]

---

1 In the first chapter of *Zen Conversations*, I present a fuller overview of the history of the transfer of Zen to North America.

Meido Moore

Meido Moore is the abbot of Korinji[2] – a Rinzai monastery in Wisconsin – and a master aikido instructor.

"I recall at a very young age, on Christmas Eve, praying for hours and working myself up into what I now recognize to be a kind of ecstatic state. So, I have that kind of nature, I guess. I hate to use the word because it has such an odd cachet these days, but I would say that I had a 'mystical' personality and was seeking some kind of experiential path. Actually, I wanted to be a Catholic priest when I was very young. But my disillusionment with Catholicism came when I realized that they didn't really get to talk to God the way that Jesus did. I understood that it was a faith-based tradition. I was seeking something more experiential."

While still in school, he came upon the Buddhist *Dhammapada*[3] which seemed grounded in that experiential approach to spirituality, and, when he enrolled at Rutgers College, he had an opportunity to go to Bodhgaya, India, the birthplace of Buddhism. There he met a number of "eminent teachers. People I had no business meeting and had no idea who they were at the time." They inspired him to enter the Buddhist path by going through the formal ritual of "Taking Refuge" in the Three Jewels (or Treasures): Buddha (the human – not divine – teacher), the Dharma (what he taught), and the Sangha (the community of those who practice his teachings).

When I ask what prompted him to take that step, he shakes his head. "I have no explanation for any of this. Honestly, it felt like a wave that was carrying me. You know, at that age we can jump into things without a lot of thought about consequences. It seemed like the right thing to do, and I did not give it a second thought. From my perspective now, I would call that some kind of karma or predilection. But at the time it just felt completely true and right, so I did it." He even considered entering an Asian monastery, but illness forced his return to the United States.

"I had dysentery from the third day in New Delhi through the four months I was in India. It was horrible. I had moments when I really thought that was it for me. I cannot say that in 1988 in Bodhgaya I was getting proper medical treatment. It's quite a different place now. But to face – as I thought – my own mortality at that age and in that way, I now recognize was an extremely valuable and profound experience. I would not trade it, but I don't want to repeat it."

---

2   "-ji" is a Japanese suffix indicating a temple, so "Korin Temple."

3   A traditional collection of the Buddha's teachings rendered in verse.

"Back at Rutgers I connected with a gentleman on campus who was a student of the Chan[4] Master Sheng Yen and ran a meditation group there. So, that led to my participating in my first Zen retreats, Chinese Zen retreats, in Queens, New York. At the same time, I started doing martial arts as a way to regain my health. I viewed it as a complementary activity to Buddhist practice. And through that I met the person who became one of my main teachers, Fumio Toyoda Sensei. He was a Japanese aikido master and also a Zen teacher connected to the lineage of Omori Sogen, a very famous Rinzai Zen master."

Within a few months of graduation, Meido moved to Chicago and took up residence in Toyoda's training hall. He remained there for the next seven years. I asked if it were a monastic environment.

"It was, and it was not. It was not what we call a *sodo*, which is a formal training monastery where people go to train to become priests. It was a Zen temple; it was a branch temple of a headquarters temple elsewhere. But it was also a martial arts training hall. It was also a place where Japanese cultural activities were going on, things like tea ceremony, flower arrangement, calligraphy, and so on. So I was in the midst of all that, and I was living essentially an ascetic or monastic lifestyle with very little sleep, long hours of training, few comforts. But I was a lay person. I was not a priest at that time.

"Because Toyoda Sensei was a Zen teacher as well as a martial arts master, to me he kind of had it all. He was a person with whom I could pursue both of those paths in unity, and that was quite exciting for me as a young man. What he was teaching was Zen and *budo*, Zen and martial arts as a unified training path. And there is certainly precedent for that, especially in Omori Sogen Roshi's[5] lineage. Omori Roshi was, arguably, the most famous Rinzai Zen Master in Japan in the 20th century, as well as a very famous sword practitioner, calligrapher, and artist. So the training system passed down in our tradition is a unified training of formal Zen – meditation, *sanzen*[6], koan practice, and so on – but also stressing the importance of some kind of physical culture, which in my case was martial arts, and some kind of fine-arts training. I was very excited about that approach. It spoke to many aspects of my character."

Meido is a man of strong opinions, which he expresses fluently. The word "Zen" has come to be used loosely in contemporary culture[7] and elements of

---

4 "Zen" is the Japanese form of the Chinese word "Chan."

5 "Roshi" is an honorific term which in Japan means "old teacher." In North American and European Zen, it has come to mean a fully qualified Zen teacher.

6 Private interviews between teacher and student. Called "dokusan" in the Soto and Sanbo Zen traditions.

7 *The Cambridge Dictionary*, for example, defines Zen as "the quality of being relaxed and not worrying about things one can't change."

Zen practice – such as meditation and mindfulness – are sometimes presented separately from their Buddhist framework. So I ask if one needs to be a Buddhist in order to practice Zen.

"No. Anyone's welcome to practice and get whatever benefit they can out of it. But if someone asks me directly, 'Do I have to be Buddhist to really grasp what Zen training is pointing at?' I'll say, 'Yes. Absolutely.' Why? Because if you remove the core Buddhist teachings and the whole intent behind the training – what the training is pointing to – then it becomes something different entirely. It becomes more of a therapeutic activity. It becomes … Well, you can see what it becomes because we have the so-called secular Buddhist movement everywhere. All the great masters, everything they've taught, the rationale behind the training – even something like the koan system – it's all pointing to the core Buddhist teachings and an experiential understanding of what those are.

"You may be familiar with the classifications that come from Guifeng Zongmi, the so-called Five Types of Zen.[8] They're all valid in as much as they give someone some benefit. But if we want to say what Zen ultimately is, it is Saijojo Zen, the highest realization and ultimately the attainment of liberation in the way that is conceived of in Buddhism. It does not mean that someone cannot do Gedo Zen or Bompu Zen for common benefit. There's no problem. Those people are welcome. But if they ask me if what they are doing is really Zen, I will tell them honestly, 'No. It's not.' *But* they're still welcome. I don't care what you call yourself. I don't need you to become any kind of -ist. I don't need you to convert to some kind of -ism unless you have the interest. But if you ask me, 'What is the intent of the training?' I will tell you from the perspective of the Buddhist teachings. What is *kensho*[9] from the perspective of the Buddhist teachings? What is the fulfillment of the post-kensho path of liberation? I will tell you from that perspective. Do you need to believe in karma and rebirth? No. You can remain agnostic about those issues, but the whole training is predicated upon it, so if you take it out, you remove a linchpin. It's fine to do that for yourself if you want. But then there is really no need to call it Zen or Buddhism anymore, is there? Just call it 'my own personal spirituality inspired

---

8   1) Bompu Zen – meditation practices undertaken for health benefit;
     2) Gedo Zen – meditation practices associated with non-Buddhist traditions;
     3) Shojo Zen – meditation practices undertaken to acquire psychological equanimity;
     4) Daijo Zen – meditation practices associated with other Mahayana Schools;
     5) Saijojo Zen – practice undertaken to achieve awakening and integrate it into one's life.

9   Awakening. Seeing into one's True Nature.

by Buddhism.' I have no problem with people getting benefit as they see fit and engaging with the tradition as they wish. What I will criticize is people who remove crucial aspects of its framework, like the Four Noble Truths,[10] for example, and still refer to it as Buddhism or Zen. You know, if you remove the teachings of karma and rebirth – someone said this; I don't recall who – the Third Noble Truth of the cessation of suffering becomes, 'You will die.' The Fourth Noble Truth, instead of revealing the Eightfold Path, becomes, 'Wait.' Because suffering will end then.

"So Buddhism is what it is. Of course, there are different expressions of it. Don't get me wrong. I understand that there is a lot of debate and creativity within it. But if someone wants to remove foundational things – as a person or an organization – that's fine. Just don't call it Buddhism. That would be the honest way to go about it. I try to present it to people this way if they ask me, 'Do I have to be Buddhist?' 'No, you don't. But I'm teaching Buddhism. Please get whatever you can get from it.

"And I leave your own mess to you,'" he adds with a chuckle.

Cynthia Kear

The largest Zen denomination in Japan is Soto, and Soto temples were founded in America long before Rinzai. They were not, however, meditation centers. They were intended to minister to the needs of immigrant populations residing on the West Coast. Sokoji in San Francisco, for example, was established in 1935 to serve about sixty Japanese families living in the area. The temple was the center of community life, a place where traditional Japanese values were retained and respected.

When Shunryu Suzuki was sent from Japan to serve as the resident priest at Sokoji in 1959, he was expected to lead Sunday services and preach sermons in an auditorium set up much like a Christian Church. There was a separate "shrine room" traditionally furnished, but there was no *zendo* or meditation hall. Zen might be the "meditation school" of Buddhism, but the temple members considered zazen[11] something for monks, not lay people.

---

10   The central Buddhist teaching:
     1) All of existence is characterized by suffering (dukkha);
     2) Suffering is caused by craving;
     3) Suffering can be ameliorated by overcoming craving;
     4) Craving can be overcome by following the Noble Eightfold path, which consists of right view, right intention, right speech, right action, right livelihood, right effort, right mindfulness, and right meditation.

11   Seated meditation.

Suzuki put up a notice inviting congregants to join him for morning mediation. None of the temple members did, but slowly a surprising group of non-Asian youth began to do so. Their numbers became so large that they had to separate from Sokoji in 1962 and incorporate as the San Francisco Zen Center, which would become the largest and wealthiest Zen Center in America.

Unlike Rinzai centers, there was little talk of enlightenment at SFZC, no koans or obscure remarks. Suzuki's instruction stressed the physical mechanics of sitting in meditation, how to place the legs and hands, how to focus the attention on the breath. When students asked questions about theory or philosophy, Suzuki side-stepped them by explaining that if he were to give them an answer they would think they understood something they did not.

Cynthia Kear is a Soto priest in the Shunryu Suzuki lineage attached to the Russian River Zendo north of San Francisco. She was raised on the East coast but after college moved across the country. "I was looking for a big change, mostly to get away from my suffering family.

"I grew up in a very dysfunctional family with lots of '-isms' – alcoholism, undiagnosed, untreated mental health – the usual kind of chaos. My father was an alcoholic. We have a lineage going back – as far as I can see – to all my ancestors having some sort of an -ism. Co-dependency. My mom was also a heavy drinker. I don't know if she was an alcoholic, but she did her best to keep up with my dad. And she certainly was a co-dependent. And, sadly, my father suffered greatly with this all the way through to the end of his life and wound up being estranged pretty much from his family and being a very isolated person who never found a way to resolve his suffering. And all of my siblings had some form of addiction. So, I thought, of course, as most people who grow up in dysfunctional families think, 'Oh, I will never be like them.'" She laughs wryly. "My drinking was wine out of very nice crystal; theirs was Budweiser out of Styrofoam coolers."

The family was Catholic. "We had priests, and we had nuns, and, by my own choice, half of my education was in Catholic schools including high school. But in my sophomore year I was introduced to the existentialists and the nihilists, and I thought, 'Oh, finally! Here's a paradigm that makes sense! Life is suffering and meaningless. Okay.' I did eventually grow out of that, but ... So after college I wanted to get away and sort of establish a different life. So I came to San Francisco."

When she was 32 she was involved in "a car accident that was definitely due to being under the influence, and I knew I needed to wake up and do something different. My youngest sister was a cocaine addict who was shipped out to me because I was the 'more stable one' – relatively speaking – and together we discovered recovery. And it was kind of like finding Buddhist practice. It was eye-opening. It was like, 'Oh, wait a second! This is not insanity. This is something very specifically that we can call a certain type of suffering. And here is the solution. Here is the medicine to wake up and transform that suffering.'"

There is a spiritual component in most recovery programs; Cynthia, however, "knew that a Judaeo-Christian paradigm was not going to work for me. Having, by my own efforts, spent a lot of time in Catholicism, patriarchy, theism, too much emphasis on an afterlife as opposed to here and now. So when I found Buddhist practice, it was like, 'Wow! Here's a solution to any other type of suffering that I have in my life.'"

She began to attend sittings at the San Francisco Zen Center but for a long while "stayed on the periphery because I thought they were all a little intimidating, and I wondered, 'Was this a cult?'

"But I loved the Dharma talks. They fed my heart and my mind.

"I think from a personal perspective, what invited me more deeply into the Dharma of the transformation of suffering was when my younger sister was dying of breast cancer. She was just my favorite person in the world; ten years younger and with little kids, and it was just so traumatizing. I was about 50 at the time. I hadn't experienced a close or a young death at that point in time. And so I clung to the Dharma. I dove into the Dharma and clung to it in terms of understanding – you know, trying to understand – with just great fervor. And I did find a lot of wisdom and, again, solace and a way of contextualizing impermanence. Then Blanche Hartman[12] was giving a Dharma talk one day. And, you know, everybody has kind of their Dharma talk that they give, and this was one of her *jukai*[13] Dharma talks. And she was talking about the etymology of 'jukai,' and that we *plunge*, we *plunge* into this life, into these vows knowing that they're impossible to take. And I'd been hanging around for three or four years, and I just thought – it was just an epiphany; it was just in that moment – 'Oh! Like a swan diving from up above off of a cliff into the ocean! That's what I want to do! I want to just plunge! And I want to keep plunging! And I never want to stop!'"

"What was the attraction?" I ask.

"Why did I want to live a life of vow? It just made so much sense to me. I mean, I found the understanding of suffering and being able to transform suffering very encouraging. I'd had two years in recovery at that point in time, and I was seeing it in other people. I was seeing in that realm that transformation of suffering was possible. So this was just kind of the next step. 'Oh! All suffering

---

12   The first woman to serve as co-Abbot at SFZC. Her term ran from 1996-2002.

13   The ceremony in which one formally vows to abide by the Buddhist Precepts. Cynthia defines jukai as "formally entering the lineage and taking the Precepts for the first time." Cf. Appendix 1.

can be transformed!' It doesn't make it easy. It doesn't make the pain go away – the sadness, the grief – but there's a way to deal with it. And it framed it in a way that the experience I was having with my sister felt both traumatic as well as personal. 'Oh! I grew up in this crazy dysfunctional family, and now my favorite person – my beautiful sister – is dying of cancer?' To sit back and to contextualize – and I don't mean to sound cold or academic here – but to just not have it be unique to me was very helpful. Many of the teachers tell us, 'There's nothing wrong here. It doesn't feel good. But this is going to happen to all of us.' It's an idea, a fixed idea, that I'm going to have 70 years or my sister's going to have 80 years or something. That's writ nowhere. So that was very helpful."

Extended residential training is central to the vision of Zen practice that Suzuki and his successors promoted. Participants are encouraged to take part in multiple ninety-day training sessions – *angos* – at the isolated Tassajara Mountain Center, the first Soto monastery to be established outside of Asia. Cynthia, however, chose to remain what is called – in Buddhist terminology – a "householder," a lay person who continues to be engaged in worldly affairs. "One reason is that when my sister died, she wanted me to take over a serious parental role with her three girls who were all under eight at the time. And I thought, 'Here's suffering.' Here is suffering that I can attend to right away. I can help these young girls. This is as valid and more meaningful for me in terms of the causes and conditions of my life than for me to go to Tassajara or some other place."

After the children became independent, Cynthia attended a number of study weeks at Tassajara and eventually came to teach there during the summers. "I love going there, and I respect and value that experience. But for me the benefit of the Dharma and the teachings of the transformation of suffering, I want to help pass that on and expose it to a much different audience. I mean, the students I work with can't afford Tassajara, can't afford taking time out to go to Tassajara. They have children, have grandchildren, have jobs, and that has never seemed inconsistent with practice. It's a different practice, but it's very much as rich as any monastic practice that I know or that I've personally experienced."

Kokyo Henkel

Early Buddhism was less a faith tradition for the general population than it was a specialized way of life for people who chose to separate themselves from the world. Similar to the Christian monastic traditions, it was a life dedicated to meditation and study. Monasticism has never been a common way of life – and is, if anything, less so now – but it is one in which Kokyo Henkel feels at home.

He first learned about Buddhism while a student at Brown University in Providence, Rhode Island. Representatives from Seung Sahn's Korean Zen temple led weekly meditation sessions on campus. "College was kind of a busy and sometimes stressful life. And I remember the first times of sitting in meditation and feeling access to a vast sense of peace and presence and simplicity walking home after the meditation and seeing the grounds of the campus so fresh and clear. I got into it quite quickly. I noticed that other students would come in and join the group for a couple of weeks and lose interest, but I just kept going.

"Also at that time, as I think many people around that age do, I started exploring psychedelics. I felt that they kind of coincided, these explorations of expanded mind states, and looking for ways to integrate those into my life more. That was an important part of my life. I think it really planted some important seeds."

After graduation, he headed to California.

"I'd heard of the San Francisco Zen Center. I didn't know anybody who practiced there, but I had their magazine, *The Wind Bell*, which was floating around my dorm in college. And it was winter when I graduated, so that was a good excuse to go to California. I took the bus, and when I got to California, I started looking for practice places. I didn't have any savings, so I was looking for places where I could work some for my stay." He discovered that such places are rare.

"But one that said, 'Yes. You can come right now' was the City of Ten Thousand Buddhas, the Chinese Chan Temple in Ukiah. I had no idea what I was getting into. It's a very traditional Chinese Buddhist monastery with maybe a couple hundred monks and nuns living there. And they were in the middle of their annual retreat, which is basically a Zen *sesshin*[14] but for three weeks. They sat from 3:00 in the morning until midnight. I had never done any retreats or anything longer than a couple of periods, but they said I could come and do some work around the place and join the retreat. It was mid-way through, and I did the last ten days of this retreat with this wonderful kind of what Suzuki Roshi called 'beginner's mind.' If I had known what it involved, I might not have gone. But it was wonderful."

He tells me it "hooked" him "at a deeper level. But at the end of the retreat, they stopped almost all silent meditation. They went into their usual daily schedule, mostly ritual chanting, and, at that time, that was all a little bit foreign to me. I wanted to find a place to do a lot of silent sitting. So by the spring I found my way to Tassajara. When I got there, that's really where I felt like I had come home, and I just stayed there. I was 23, and I spent the next twenty years there and at Green Gulch, which is kind of a semi-monastic farm

---

14   A Zen retreat, traditionally seven days long.

community up in the Marin hills. So I spent the next twenty years between those two temples. Basically I grew up there and went through many changes over those twenty years. I also traveled to Asia, like a pilgrimage through India and later China, and I spent almost a year in Japan at Bukkokuji monastery."

He eventually was appointed Head of Practice at Tassajara, a position he held until he was asked to be the resident priest for a Zen community in Santa Cruz. When I met Kokyo, his term at Santa Cruz was just ending, and he was planning to go to on a three-month retreat in Colorado because a former plan to move to Nepal had been prevented by the pandemic. He admitted that he had felt more at home in Tassajara than he had in Santa Cruz.

"I have such a love for sesshin and retreats and deep Dharma study. The monastic routine involves lots of zazen and ritual forms and work practice and community life. And with all of that at Tassajara I really felt like I could access a kind of peace and contentment, an acceptance of myself and others. And living more in the present, less caught up in all the ideas of what I was 'supposed' to be doing with my life. As I continued through the years of monastic life, the peacefulness kept growing. I think the original impetus was just to straighten out my crazy mind a little bit, but that gradually developed into more of a *bodhicitta*[15] aspiration: 'Oh! There's infinite potential for benefitting self and others in this practice.' And the other things I was interested in my life – in possibly doing afterwards – became less interesting compared to the Zen practice. The longer I stayed, the more I wanted to stay and continue doing it. So after a few years at Tassajara I became a priest."

"What does that mean in your tradition?" I ask. "If you were in a Training Center like Bukkokuji in Japan, for example, you'd be preparing to take over a temple somewhere. You kind of did that in Santa Cruz but admitted it wasn't necessarily a good fit. So what is the role of a priest in the San Francisco lineage?"

"Yeah. It's never been so clearly defined actually. But it is a long-term, ideally a lifetime, commitment to put the practice – the formal practice of zazen and the rituals and Dharma study – at the center of one's life. That's how I think of it. That was the motivation for me to be ordained. And also the more I practiced and studied the Buddhadharma, and the more I read of the example of Shakyamuni Buddha, which was so inspiring to me, the life of renunciation and simplicity became more of an aspiration, really letting go of anything in my life that would pull me away from this heartfelt calling to just practice Buddha's way."

"Is there an assumption that ordination implies some sort of service to the community?" I ask.

---

15   The intention to achieve awakening for the benefit of others.

"Yes. Especially in San Francisco Zen Center, when living in those residential communities like Tassajara and Green Gulch. Actually everybody who's living there is serving the community in that way, but the priests may have a higher expectation placed on them to really say 'yes' to everything and help out however possible and eventually start teaching others. So it is a life of service, for sure."

"That's service to the sangha," I note. "Is there a sense of obligation to serve the wider community?"

"Well, it's interesting living in a place like Tassajara, which is a remote mountain monastery. For some of us who lived there for many years, we hardly ever even left the monastery. It was difficult to leave, and you were only supposed to leave once a month to go into town if you had to see a doctor or something. And no internet either. But people came in. So the world was invited into the monastery, especially in summer, which was 'guest season,' when thousands of people would come through to stay there. So in a way we were serving the larger community – often the non-Buddhist community – in this unusual way, not so much going out into it but inviting the community in. Tassajara turns into a kind of hot springs rustic vacation community in the summer. It's still trying to keep the monastic framework, but there are many, many people coming in, and there was a feeling of serving that way. Since all beings are caught in the suffering of *samsara*, they are all in need of help."

John Pulleyn

A Zen boom took place in North America during the late '60s and early '70s made up primarily of young people who found their way to places like the San Francisco Zen Center, many of them inspired by a book published in 1965 which described a very different form of Zen than Shunryu Suzuki was presenting.

The Three Pillars of Zen, compiled and edited – with assistance – by Philip Kapleau, consists of a series of introductory lectures given by the Japanese Zen master, Haku'un Yasutani, a teisho by Yasutani on the koan *Mu,*[16] transcripts of private interviews with students in *dokusan* – something which had never previously been available in any language – and the personal accounts of eight lay practitioners, Japanese and American, who had achieved kensho.

Yasutani was the Dharma Heir of Daiun Harada Roshi, a Soto priest who – because he had been dissatisfied with the level of insight he had acquired from traditional Soto practice – studied with several Rinzai masters as well. He

---

16   The koan commonly given to beginning students: A monk asks the 9th century master, Joshu, "Does a dog have Buddha-nature?" Joshu replied, "*Mu!*" Mu literally means "no" or "nothing."

eventually attained awakening under their guidance and became an advocate for the koan system more commonly associated with Rinzai Zen. He combined elements of both traditions in his own teaching. After Harada died, Yasutani formally broke with the Soto establishment and initiated an independent school, the Sanbo Kyodan, or the Fellowship of the Three Treasures,[17] modeled on Harada's approach. Both Yasutani and Harada feared that Zen was on the wane in Japan. After the humiliation of military defeat in World War II, large numbers of young Japanese had turned away from the political, cultural, and religious structures – including Buddhism – they blamed for involving them in the war. Soto monasteries were falling into ritualism and rote training for priests who were often young men responsible for maintaining a family-run temple but who had no real interest in doing so. Yasutani decided, instead, to focus on lay practitioners – including foreigners like Kapleau – rather than monks.

The emphasis of *The Three Pillars of Zen* is on the physical and mental mechanics of zazen. There were many books available on Zen in the West by the mid-60s, but none of them provided information about *how* to meditate. Kapleau dismissed the lot as "a pseudo-Zen which is little more than a mind-tickling diversion of highbrows and a plaything of beatniks."[18] These books, he stated, clogged the mind "with splinters of koans and irrelevant fragments of philosophy, psychology, theology, and poetry which churn about"[19] in the brain ultimately creating an impediment to genuine Zen practice. *The Three Pillars of Zen*, on the other hand, was "nothing less than a manual of self-instruction."[20]

In San Francisco, Shunryu Suzuki seldom talked about enlightenment and taught his students to practice without expectations. In contrast, kensho was all important in Kapleau's understanding of Zen, as it had been to Harada and Yasutani. Without enlightenment, Kapleau declared in his outspoken manner, Zen practice was meaningless.

John Pulleyn is Co-Director of the Rochester Zen Center established by Kapleau a year after he published *The Three Pillars*.

John learned about Zen while a student at Oberlin College in Ohio. Oberlin hadn't been his first choice. "I foolishly only applied to two schools, Harvard and Swarthmore. Didn't get into either one of them. I was a poor interview because I was so awkward and shy, which I think is why I didn't get in even though my guidance counselor told me, 'Oh, you'll get into any school

---

17   In 2014, the school was renamed Sanbo Zen.
18   *The Three Pillars of Zen*, p. xv.
19   Ibid. 87.
20   Ibid. *xvi*.

you want to.' My grades were almost perfect, and my SAT scores were very high. So I cast about and ended up getting an invitation to go to Oberlin."

"And you graduated," I said.

"I did."

"And afterwards?"

"I went to Rochester and started practicing Zen."

"Okay, let's back up and fill in a few gaps."

He explains that the summer before he graduated in 1968, a friend invited him and some other friends to come up to his parents' place in Vermont where "we were mostly smoking dope and going to hippie gatherings. And we were taking a walk in the woods, and I noticed a mushroom, one of those shelf mushrooms growing out of a tree trunk, and I said, 'That's disgusting.' And my friend said, 'Well, you know, Alan Watts[21] would say that it's your mind that's disgusting.' And for whatever reason, that just went right on target. I just went, 'Whoa! That's right.' So at that point I started reading all the Alan Watts that I could lay my hands on. When I went back to Oberlin for that final semester, I went up into the stacks and there was C.C. Chang's *The Practice of Zen* and some of those other early books. I was reading along, and then a friend of mine had stolen *The Three Pillars of Zen* from the Oberlin College bookshop. He lent it to me, and that was it. 'Cause I'd been looking for how do you meditate. And there was very, very little mention of that. I read all of D.T. Suzuki, and he really wasn't talking about it. Alan Watts certainly didn't talk about it. I did find one book that had a description of how to do *metta* meditation from a Southeast Asian tradition, so I tried it."

"A loving-kindness meditation?" I ask.

"Yeah. I can't remember what the instructions were, but I had a really interesting experience. It was time for me to go do my job – I washed pots in one of the dormitories after meals – I went off to do that. And everybody I ran into, the cooks in the cafeteria and whatnot, everybody was just in a wonderful frame of mind. I couldn't understand how it happened. But what's amazing to me looking back on it is that I never did that meditation again. 'Wow! That was weird.' And went onto whatever else I was doing; I can't remember what. The other thing I was doing a lot of in college was smoking pot and looking for any opportunity to take peyote or acid."

He was also a heavy drinker. "I'm built for alcohol. It's in my family on both sides. My body tolerates it well, and it fixes what's wrong, or it seemed to for quite a while."

Before graduating from Oberlin, he phoned the Rochester Center. "And I

---

21 Watts was a popular writer on Zen and other Asian spiritual topics.

got Roshi Kapleau on the phone. So it was a very small operation then. And he said, 'Well, there are lots of jobs in Rochester. Just come on up.' So I did that. Took a bus from Toledo to Rochester. Got a room at the YMCA, and then went for my interview with Roshi Kapleau.

"I remember at some point he asked me what my aspiration was. And I remember putting my arm on the back of the couch and saying, 'Well, I want to come to awakening. I think I want to come to awakening. But maybe I'm kidding myself.' You know, thinking this was where I wanted to go, but I just didn't know what I was doing? And I explained I was at the Y and needed a place to say. So he said, 'Well, there are a lot of places you could rent just around here.' He took me outside – it was February – and we started walking down the street and just going up to houses, knocking on the door, and when somebody came to the door, he said, 'This young man has come to study with me. Do you have any rooms to rent?' We didn't find any, but I was just so struck by that, because I was still a pretty shy kid, and the idea of walking up to somebody's house and asking that was just amazing."

He eventually found a place through the classified ads in the newspaper.

"After I'd been in Rochester a little while, people started to pour in. The composition of the center changed; I was there when the change happened."

He regularly attended sittings at the center and worked at a temp agency "that used to hire people to sweep out warehouses or just menial jobs. You didn't get paid a lot, but we didn't need very much money. People don't realize that the equation was different back then. You could rent a room for $10 a week, and we were living on rice and soybeans and buying tomato soup on sale. And it was fine.

"I have never dropped my Zen Center membership – so I've been a member for over fifty years – but there came a point where I was really ... stuck, I guess. It seemed really hard, and maybe I was unconsciously looking for some way out. And I had gotten married, and we had a child, and I'd also rekindled my fondness for alcohol and was drinking fairly frequently. I was also aware of a lot of things that were wrong with the center – you know, people's pretentions – and I just sort of drifted away."

"What kind of pretentions?" I asked.

"Well, here's a little story that'll kind of give you the flavor of it. At some point, the local movie theater was showing samurai films, *Seven Samurai* or some other Kurosawa movie, and everybody went including Roshi. And the next day, at morning zazen every young guy who walked in was doing the samurai walk. You know?" He demonstrates by walking wide-legged and rolling his shoulders. "And then Roshi Kapleau came in, and he was just Roshi Kapleau moseying in."

"So you took a break."

"I did, though I didn't know I was doing that. I went from being on-staff and sort of in the middle of things to being on the periphery. Just coming for sittings. I did do a few sesshins even then, and they were all hard. And I remember there was one sesshin when my wife and I had an apartment on Goodman Street, and – I guess this was just after our first child was born – and I was going to sesshin the next day, walking across Goodman Street, and I remember wishing, 'Wouldn't it be great if a car would hit me.' You know, to take me out of this situation that I'm in. So emotionally I was really looking for some way out.

"So I never dropped my membership. I just wasn't there, and I was drinking a lot and smoking dope and" – he sighs – "deeply enjoying my unpretentious life. Every now and then I'd go back, and then at some point a friend of mine – who was also in a similar position to me having been at the center but not doing a lot then – he wanted to go back and do a sitting, and I went with him. This was in the late '80s. And I remember running into people I knew from back in the day, and them saying, 'Look at how it's all changed. All these people are different and whatnot.'

"But what really turned the corner for me, was in 1990, on August 23rd, I was stopped for driving under the influence in a black out. And one thing led to another. I had to talk to a lawyer, and he told me I would need to get an evaluation. The judge would want to see that. So I went for an alcohol evaluation, and I told them, 'Well, what I'll do from here on in, I'll only drink one or two beers a night.' And they laughed – 'Ha, ha, yeah, right' – and my wife was with me, and she said, 'You know, he can do that.' I had a lot of willpower for the stuff I wanted to do. But they said, 'Well, we would still recommend that you stop drinking and that you do treatment.' And I said, 'Well, I'll think about it.' And then I had a physical with my doctor, and I told him the situation and that they wanted me to do treatment, and he said, 'Think about it this way. You'll learn stuff about alcoholism.' That sort of flipped a switch. I thought, 'Yeah. That'd be interesting. I'll do it.' And I think they were surprised when I came back and said, 'Yes. I'll do the program.' And that ... that was amazing. Almost immediately I loved it.

"The first thing that's amazing is these people aren't pretentious. Everybody's been levelled. You're starting with the first step; we admitted we were powerless and that our lives had become unmanageable. It was *sooo* different from trying to live up to the level of an ancient Zen Master and sort of present yourself as some lightning rod for spirituality. So, I was on a pink cloud. I remember driving around Rochester thinking, 'This whole town is full of church basements. Full of people meeting.' It was amazing to be in a room and think, 'What's with this guy?' You know, he's just slumped in his chair, he looks bored, and why is he even here? And then he'd open his mouth and speak and tell you something that was really, really helpful. So I was just enjoying that."

At the completion ceremony when the mandated program ended, the facilitator had final words of advice for each of the participants. "And she said to me, 'I think you need to go back to the Zen Center.' Because I'd obviously talked about it although I can't remember what I said. And meditation's a big part of the AA program. So I knew I was going back. It was pretty clear, that's where I needed to go."

He resumed regular sitting and attending sesshin and after another fourteen years on the periphery went back on staff. "So I was just an active member of the center until 2003, when I got roped into being Head of Zendo. And even then I didn't go back as a resident, but I started being there every day."

Scott Thornton

In North American Zen, the Rochester Zen Center, established by Philip Kapleau, rivals SFZC in prominence, and Kapleau's importance in establishing the practice in the West cannot be overstated. Still, he is a controversial figure. He and Yasutani had a falling out, after which Yasutani no longer acknowledged Kapleau as a student, thereby casting doubt on his authority to teach. The Sanbo Zen tradition still doesn't recognize him as part of their lineage and questions his right to claim authorship of *The Three Pillars of Zen*. They point out that the book was the work of three people, Kapleau and two others he identifies as his "collaborators" in the Editor's Preface – Koun Yamada and Akira Kubota – but whose names do not appear on the title page. Koun Yamada was Yasutani's immediate successor as abbot of the Sanbo Zen tradition.

The Sanbo Zen hub center in the United States is the beautifully constructed Mountain Cloud Zen Center in Santa Fe which – ironically – had been built by members of the Rochester community. The intention had been that Kapleau would retire to Santa Fe, but circumstances required him to return to New York. Over time, the membership of Mountain Cloud dispersed until only a handful of people remained. Will Brennan is given credit for keeping the center alive without the aid of a resident teacher for more than twenty years until he recruited a recently authorized Sanbo Zen teacher, Henry Shukman,[22] to come to Santa Fe.

Henry explains that Sanbo Zen differs from other Zen schools in a couple of ways. "Sanbo Zen is lay, meaning that we don't do ordination. There are a very few who are ordained; in order to be a teacher in Sanbo Zen you don't

---

22   Cf. *Zen Conversations*, pp. 40-41, 60-63, 85-86, 108-09.

have to be ordained. And Sanbo Zen is rather narrow in its focus, which is basically on the awakening process through koan training."[23]

Henry remains the Spiritual Director of Mountain Cloud, but he is now assisted by Valerie Forstman who has taken on the role of guiding teacher. Her husband, Scott Thornton, has also recently been designated an assistant teacher. I ask him what that authorizes him to do.

"What I understand in the really formal sense is that basically what I can do is instruct people in meditation and little else. But 'the times they are a-changin' – you know? – and there seems to be a need for more people who aren't quite at the teacher level. There's just many more students coming than the teachers can handle."

Scott grew up in Memphis, Tennessee, and a trace of his old accent still colors his speech.

"We were Baptists. My mother was very devout. My father went along for the ride."

"And you?"

"At one point, I was a pretty reverent kid. I got a little irreverent in my adolescence. By then the tenets of the church didn't hold together for me anymore, so I just sort of eased out. I never declared, 'I'm not a Baptist,' but I just kind of eased out and quit going to church."

He tells me he felt a lot of anger as a young person. "I can remember being an angry kid. I actually remember being about eight years old and realizing, 'You don't smile, man.' It was like I never smiled. It wasn't like 'rage anger,' but it was just this internal tension that I associate with exactly how my mother was. I'm a psychologist, and they say we do anger the way our mothers did. So, I don't know. I do anger the way she would suppress ..." He grimaces, tightens his body and speaks in a strained voice imitating his mother's way of talking when she was upset: "'Rrrrr! I don't like the way he acts! Why do people have to be this way? Rrrr!' It was like that."

The anger abated a little when he started college. "I felt really liberated when I left home and went to college, even though I commuted to college right there in Memphis. Still I spent a lot more time away from home. So my best analysis of where that anger came from is good old Freudian repression. Sexual repression. My mother was a really repressed person. And my father drank, and she hated that. So there was tension in the household that I did not like. There are still residues of that old anger in me, and on rare occasions it can suddenly rise up. That's a poison, as we know, from Buddhist sutras. My effort now is not to fight it, but to give it the space needed to be soothed. If handled like that, the

---

[23] Email correspondence with the author and Diane Fitzgerald (cf. *Zen Conversations*), October 4, 2021.

poisons can be our teachers."[24]

He discovered meditation through theatre. "I was in the first college production of the musical *Hair*.[25] And Claude – the lead character – meditates at the beginning of the play. He comes out and sits down with kind of an Indian blanket around himself and just sits there for – oh – about fifteen/twenty minutes before the show starts, and the cast kind of gradually starts sort of meandering through the audience and comin' around and finally the music picks up. So I acted like I was meditating, and, in retrospect, I was meditating. I mean, it was just …"

"What else was there to do?"

"Yeah. So I never meditated but I played a meditator on stage. And then a couple of years later there was this book, *A Child's Garden of Grass*.[26] And there was one section in there about, 'Can Grass Enhance Meditation? Yes!' So I tried it. They were debunking TM,[27] I think. They said, 'You can pay a lot of money to some guru who will give you a "secret mantra" or here's a free one.' And I remember it! As you breathe in, 'oon'; as you breath out, 'yellimon.' And so I practiced, 'oon/yellimon' quite often. And then I abandoned that. But then in 1988, I remember the moment. I had been Christmas shopping a few months earlier, and I bought a book called *How to Meditate*.[28] I was going to give it to a friend, but I started reading it, and I just kept it. And it kinda simmered there in the background for a while. Then I remember this moment. My wife and I were remodeling our house, and it was a construction site. I had just got licensed as a psychologist about two weeks prior, and I was just having one of these, 'Is this all there is?' moments. And so I sat on top of a pile of construction material in my backyard in March and started counting my breath. The book gave about eighty techniques, but that was the one that caught me for some reason. So I practiced breath counting for twelve years really, really regularly. And it morphed into what I called, 'Listening to the Sounds of the World.' I became absorbed in sound. My stepdaughter, meanwhile, had been

---

24 Buddhist theory identifies three fundamental "poisons" at the root of human suffering: ignorance, greed, and aversion/anger.

25 *Hair: An American Tribal Love-Rock Musical* ran on Broadway in the lates 1960s. It promoted a hippie lifestyle and resistance to the Vietnam War.

26 *The Official Handbook for Marijuana Users* by Jack Margolis and Richard Clorfene, published in 1969.

27 Transcendental Meditation, a Hindu-based form of mantra recitation popular in the 1960s.

28 By Lawrence LeShan, published 1974,

going to Maria Kannon, Ruben Habito's[29] Zen Center, and I finally read *Three Pillars of Zen*, and she said, 'Hey, Scott, we got this place over here.' And that's when I hooked up with Ruben in 2000."

I ask him what Zen practice does.

"Zen is a way of meditating which brings us closer and closer to what you might call your true self. And it's a journey, and it's a process, but also every time you do it, that's it. Zen is an action."

"How does it bring you closer to your true self?"

He sits quietly for a while, then tells me a story.

"Yeah. Just my own experience: There's a fire, let's say, of anxiety or a fire of anger that's … call it a six. At a level six. In my own life, in my functioning, when I came to Zen, I had been doing the breath counting and had a regular solo practice with deep moments of absorption which were lovely. And I think they made me more appreciative of being alive. But I remember my first sesshin after about maybe three months of practice at Maria Kannon. And I'm sitting around in this circle before we start, and they say, 'What's your aspiration? What's your intention? What do you want to get out of this sesshin?' And I said, 'I'd really like to clear out some of this anger that I walk around with.' They said, 'That's good; that's good.'

"So I had a really, really good time. I was a total beginner and no expectations, and just jumped right into it. I had a couple of amazing moments. And on the way home – this was in Fort Worth and I'm in Dallas, and that's about a forty-five-mile drive through this sprawling metroplex with horrible traffic and everything – and I was just in love with every car, every building. You know? And when I got home, my wife – she died about nine years ago – but she and I had been married some twenty-five years at that point, I guess. And it was a good relationship, but we had a lot of spats; we fought a lot. And I came home, and she was not real thrilled that I'd gone away for this retreat, and she just felt totally abandoned. So we had a big ol' squabble as soon as I got home. And I remember this moment when it just fell out of me, this anger just … I can't explain it. It just dropped. And I went and sat for about an hour. And I came back, and I think I apologized for whatever my part in it was. I didn't care if she apologized or not. This sense of love replaced where the anger had been. And we never had another fight the next nine years. I mean, that was it."

---

29 Cf. *Zen Conversations*, pp. 83-84; 127.

David Weinstein

Most Zen Centers in the West are smaller than either Rochester or San Francisco. The majority have fewer than three or four dozen members. Many of the teachers working with these communities trace their authorization back to a handful of pioneers who established the tradition in the West. John Tarrant[30] – a second generation descendent of Koun Yamada – is one of the most prolific of those ancestors.

David Weinstein is one of Tarrant's heirs. He is the Director of the Rockridge Meditation Community in Oakland, California, and a Supervising Teacher in Tarrant's Pacific Zen Institute.

After completing a psychology degree at the University of Nevada in 1973, he went to Europe and Asia. "Travelling was part of my practice, though I didn't formally have a meditation practice. Travelling from country to country, experiencing the rules being so different helped weaken my self-cherishing thoughts. 'This is the way they do it here. You don't eat with the left hand, and what I think is correct is not correct here.' It loosened up my idea of what's right and wrong. Who I am. All of the stuff that a meditation practice does. Travelling has been an important teacher."

He eventually went to Nepal. "I had heard the hash was cheap, and I loved tall mountains, so I thought smoking cheap hash in the Himalayas was nirvana basically."

A friend had told him about two monks – Lamas Yeshe and Zopa – with whom they'd done a meditation course in Nepal. So, David made his way to Kopan Monastery outside of Kathmandu. "It turned out that the meditation course was actually a meditation retreat. I thought I was going to hear academic lectures about meditation, instead it was wake up at four in the morning and start meditating and continue meditating until late at night. Some people were doing full prostrations, which struck me as weird. I didn't want to do full-length prostrations, and no one said I had to. I was told to pay attention to what was going on in my experience sitting there not doing them. Eventually, I started doing them as an experiment. Lama Yeshe said, 'Try it out as an experiment. See what happens.' So, I thought, 'I've never done a prostration before, I'll try it out; see what happens.' I found that it was yet another *upaya*, another skillful means, that helped me be able to just be with my mind. Offering incense, lighting candles, having an altar, all of that arranging of the contingencies of reinforcement around me made lots of sense to me. My advisor in the psychology department had been a Skinnerian Behaviorist, and meditation seemed

---

30   Cf. *Zen Conversations*, pp. 86-87.

like, 'Oh, this is how we take control of the contingencies around us that are impinging on our mind, fostering the cultivation of unskillful mind habits. We can change those habits just like we change the behavior of animals running through a maze.' I once asked Lama Yeshe if he knew what brainwashing was. He said, 'Oh, yes.' And I said, 'Well, I feel like I'm brainwashing myself.' And he said, 'Very good. Carry on.'

"One of the western monks would lead us through guided meditations that involved visualizations and mantra practice with a little bit of just empty space. My mind needed all that stuff to give it something to chew on. If I'd walked into a Zen Center at that point in my life and someone said, 'Sit down, turn around, and shut up' – a typical instruction – I wouldn't have been able to do it."

Eventually his travels brought him to Hawaii. "I had gotten the address of the Koko An Zendo from someone at Kopan, so I thought I'd check it out." Koko An had been founded by Robert Aitken, one of the earliest American Zen pioneers and John Tarrant's teacher.

"At that time, I was doing a hybrid of Zen and Tibetan practice. I had started Zen practice in Bodhgaya, actually. I'd gone there for the Tibetan New Year teachings by the Dalai Lama. I was expecting a solemn event with important religious teachings, but it turned out to be more like a county fair with Tibetans from all over the sub-continent. Having done a one-month solitary retreat at the Lamas' retreat center in Dharamsala after the three months of retreat at Kopan, I wasn't into all the hubbub. I found myself going as far away from the noise as I could get, which was the Japanese temple on the edge of town. The bare white walls and plain wood, the simplicity of the Japanese Temple felt like a breath of fresh air after my time in the almost psychedelic imagery of the Tibetan tradition. Lama Yeshe was in Bodhgaya at the time, and I went to talk to him as I was concerned that taking up a Zen practice might create confusion and negatively affect my Tibetan practice. He said, 'Oh, very good. Zen practice is like Tibetan Mahamudra practice. You go practice Zen. No problem.'

In Honolulu, David was accepted into the graduate program in the Religion Department of the University of Hawaii and given a job as a teaching assistant.

"I wanted a community to practice with and had to choose between Tibetan or Zen. I went to Koko An and to the nearby Tibetan Center. I felt more comfortable at Koko An, where John Tarrant was the house manager at the time."

He remained with the community for three years. "Then I had the opportunity to go to Japan to research a form of psychotherapy based on Zen called Morita Psychotherapy." In Japan, he continued his Zen practice with Aitken's teacher, Yamada Koun.

"I'd met him once in Hawaii when he came through town and stopped off at the zendo to give a talk. A group of us went to dinner with him before his talk. The waitress came and took our order, and then there was a little pause, and she said, 'To drink?' There was a deafening silence. Normally I would have had a beer even though we were going to meditate later. But nobody ordered a beer. Yamada finally broke the silence and said, 'Well, aren't you going to have something to drink?' One of the members of the group said, 'Well, Roshi, we're going to meditate after this; we probably shouldn't drink.' The Roshi laughed and said, 'Our minds are always under the influence of something. Drink, if you want to.' Everybody breathed a sigh of relief and ordered Tsingtao beer. When the waitress came to Yamada, he said, 'Tea.' He chose caffeine over alcohol.

"I immediately liked Yamada, but when I got to Japan, though I loved meditation, I was not practicing with koans. So, in my first meeting with Yamada in Kamakura, he listened to me tell him that I didn't sit with koans but rather practiced *shikan taza*.[31] I felt I had to tell him the truth, as I had with Aitken Roshi. I was prepared for him to kick me out, but instead he said, 'Shikan taza is a very difficult practice. Not many people attain realization with shikan taza. Maybe the last person to attain realization with shikan taza was … mmm … Dogen.[32] But, I want you to attain realization with shikan taza. Please practice diligently.' You could have knocked me over with a feather. Then he asked me a question; he said, 'I have this question to ask you. I don't want you to think about it. You know, just forget it.' And he asked me how to stop the sound of the distant temple bell. Which I didn't know was a koan.

"It's hard for me to say I took up the koan. It feels more like I dropped it down or swallowed it or something. Because he told me not to think about the question, I didn't. It didn't make sense to me and not thinking about it was just fine with me. Nonetheless, my practice changed. It became less rigid. Maybe that was something to do with the koan. It certainly had something to do with having felt seen by Yamada in a way I never had before. It allowed me to be open when he asked me about the question, as he did from time to time. I didn't feel on the spot or anxious about responding. It was like, 'No, I have nothing to say.' He'd say, 'Oh? Okay.'"

In this gentle manner, Yamada introduced David to koan practice.

He was in Kamakura for seven years. He met the woman he later married there and felt settled, but he didn't want to remain an English language instructor. "I had volunteered to be a crisis counselor on the Tokyo English Lifeline, a

---

31 Shikan taza – or "just sitting" – uses simple awareness as a meditation practice. The meditator does not have a particular focus, such as the breath or a koan.

32 Dōgen Zenji, the 13th Japanese who brought Soto [Caodong] Zen to Japan. Much of contemporary Soto teaching in America is based on Dogen's writing.

telephone crisis call service, and my experience there had confirmed my desire to do that kind of work. At the time you could make a pretty good living as an English-language therapist in Tokyo because there were so many multinational corporations with staff there. They'd displaced entire families and moved them to Tokyo, and work in marriage and family therapy was booming because the families were falling apart under the stress. I figured I could get my license quickly in California and then return to Tokyo, set up my practice, and live happily ever after, practicing Zen with Yamada. I started to apply to schools narrowing it down to the Naropa Institute in Boulder or the California Institute of Integral Studies in San Francisco. When I heard that John Tarrant had moved from Honolulu to Santa Rosa, that decided it for me. I knew John and liked him. Although I hadn't experienced him as a teacher, I found myself happy to entertain that as a possibility."

David had gone through the koans of the *Mumonkan* and the *Blue Cliff Record* with Yamada by the time he came to California, but when he met with Tarrant, "John said, 'Let's start from the beginning.' I had two thoughts when he made that suggestion. First was, 'Oh no!' and the second, 'Wow, that's great. Let's do that.' So, we went all the way back to the beginning of what we call the Miscellaneous Koans, and it was fantastic. It was a way for us to reconnect with each other and also get a sense of what koan practice was for each of us."

To support himself while doing his Master's degree, he worked as a guide for Japanese tourists. "But when the 1989 earthquake happened, the tour guide business dropped off because of the reduction in Japanese coming to San Francisco. So I was laid off and started going through the process of applying to collect unemployment insurance. It was a very frustrating experience. In the middle of one of those frustrating days, the koan I had been hanging out with came to life for me. When I was in Japan with Yamada, if I brought him stories of koans coming alive in my life, he would listen and nod his head and say, 'Yes, well, now, back to the koan.' I came to understand that he didn't work that way. So, I stopped bringing those experiences to him, and that was okay because I loved him and accepted him for who he was as he had accepted me.

"Then this experience happened, and I thought, 'What the hell, I'll bring it to John and see what he does with it.' And it was … I don't know … It was electric. I told him what happened, and we looked at each other, and it was like: what would it be like if we explored koans with people in a way that not only sought the traditional responses but also required people to find the koan in their life, to present the koan from the material of their life? What would that be like?

"In Kamakura when people 'finished' koan practice there was a ceremony. I witnessed a number of those ceremonies, usually people who had been practicing for 40 years or so. During those ceremonies, Yamada said the same thing, 'Now the real work begins. The integration of the practice into your life.' I always thought that it was odd to wait, but that's the way it was. What we're experimenting with is growing a culture that supports the integration of the practice in our life from the get-go."

Judy Roitman

In addition to Japanese Zen, there are schools in the West which originated in China, Korea, and Vietnam as well.

Judy Roitman and her husband, Stan Lombardo, are the founding teachers of the Kansas Zen Center in the Kwan Um School of Zen. Kwan Um is a Korean lineage established by Master Seung Sahn. It was the school Kokyo Henkel encountered when at Brown University.

Judy has the official title of Zen Master in the Kwan Um school, which puts her fairly high in their current hierarchy of teachers. Her first encounter with Buddhism, however, wasn't auspicious. "In my senior year at Sarah Lawrence College, it was advertised that a Buddhist monk would come and give a lecture. It turned out he was Tibetan. I didn't know what he was at the time because I knew nothing about Buddhism. He had the one-shoulder robe, and he was accompanied by an American guy also wearing the same kind of robe, and the American was very hairy. And the other guy – the teacher – his facial skin was so tight he was like a mummy. And the American attendant/translator looked like a Marine. And they're just sitting there as everyone's coming in. The way I tell this story is I'm from New York; I'd never seen anyone sit still, and that's actually sort of true. And I was just completely freaked out by these people. The deal was, you'd write a question, and then you'd put it in a little basket, and then they'd open them up sort of randomly and pick one out and answer it. And the answers didn't make sense. In my memory somebody would ask something like, 'Is there life after death?' And the teacher would respond with something like, 'A butterfly lands on a flower.' The answers had nothing to do with the questions, so I was getting really freaked out by this, seriously freaked out. I reached a point where I couldn't sit there anymore, and I walked out. And when I got out of the building, I started screaming. That's how affected I was."

It seemed unlikely, at the time, that she would have anything more to do with Buddhism; however, she had some personal challenges after leaving Sarah Lawrence.

"I'd had an emotionally very difficult childhood, and suddenly it was all coming out. I was so angry I didn't know I was angry. I was over-bearing; I was unpleasant. I didn't have a sense of proportion. I was delusional. I was suicidal. I was just sort of weird and strange and deeply, deeply unhappy. To soothe myself, I was a binge eater; if I'd known about bulimia, I would have thrown up. That had started my freshman year in college, but I stopped binge eating by becoming a smoker my second year in college and immediately lost a whole bunch of weight and became a chain-smoker. But then I stopped smoking, and I became a binge eater again. I was deeply, deeply miserable. And I called up this woman – back then you'd call up shrinks and they would actually answer the phone themselves – and so I would call these people up and say, 'I need an appointment.' And it was, 'Well, I have an appointment in six months; I have an appointment in three months.' And so I called this woman. She goes, 'I have an appointment in six weeks.' Then she goes, 'Is this an emergency?' And I said, 'Yes! Yes! It's an emergency!' 'Oh, okay. I can see you next week.' She saved my life.

"I was very intellectual. I really lived up in my frontal lobes. And with regular shrinks, which I'd had since I was 15, I knew how to dance and step aside and never really look at what I needed to look at. But this person was a Gestalt shrink. I don't know if you know anything about Gestalt technique, but here's an example. One time I walked in her office, and I said, 'I actually remembered a dream.' 'Oh, great. Tell me about it.' 'Okay, so I'm walking down this road.' And she says, 'Oh. What's it like to be the road?' I said, 'No! That's not what my dream is about.' And she says, 'Well, tell me about the road.' 'The road. Let's see. It's made of asphalt, and it's grey, and everybody walks on it, and *nobody loves me!*' It's like *kong-ans*.[33] They get you from the side. You know? You don't see it coming. So you can't dance around it.

"Just before I started seeing her, I saw an article in the *New York Times* on relaxation response meditation. And I grabbed that and started doing relaxation response meditation. I worked with this therapist, and I did relaxation response meditation for about two years. Then one day I was in her office, and I looked at her, and I said, 'I don't have to be this way, do I?' And she said, 'No, you don't.' And it lifted, like a tornado. It was just gone. I still get unhappy and angry, but that hint of insanity, that skewed vision, that weird kind of distortion that colors everything, that was gone. It was just absolutely amazing.

"That's when I decided I could meditate with a group. Before that, I just couldn't do it. I was too unstable, too self-absorbed. But then I thought, 'Okay, now I can go sit with a group.' So I was living in Cambridge, and I would take walks, and there was this beautiful Zen Center that I would walk by. It was just beautiful. Broad manicured lawn and a beautiful old building gorgeously

---

33   The Korean term for "koan."

maintained. So I looked up Cambridge Zen Center, and I discovered it was in Allston. And I thought, 'That's weird. I guess they moved.' And, of course, it was a different Zen center. But I didn't know that. So I walked into this funky old building and Mark Houghton – who later became a teacher – and the woman he was married to at the time, Dyan Eagles – who is also a teacher now – they were in long robes and were chasing each other around with little brass plant sprayers. And Larry Rosenberg, who later became a *Vipassana*[34] teacher, was in the kitchen, washing the dishes with another guy, Peter Harrington, and I just felt like, 'Oh, these are my people.' I walked into the kitchen and one of either Larry or Peter said, 'Well, what practice do you do?' And I said, 'Well, I count my breaths.' And Peter whirls around and said, 'How many have you counted?' And I just thought, 'I'm home!'"

"Then we went into the Dharma room, Peter hit this big bell and did this bell chant, and — I'm the daughter and granddaughter of cantors — I just felt, 'I'm home!' I never looked for any other type of practice. Later as a mature student I would practice with other people because I was curious about the teachers, and also part of our transmission process is you have to practice outside of our school. But in that moment I just felt, 'I'm home' and never seriously looked for another practice.

"I had to hold myself back. I couldn't practice in the morning because of my teaching schedule. So I limited myself. 'Only two nights a week, you can only go two nights a week.' Because a part of me was ready to shave my head and run off to Korea, but I didn't. I found Master Seung Sahn's Cambridge Zen center in my last year in Boston. And I took Precepts[35] very quickly. I first went there on Yom Kippur, October 6, 1976, and I took Precepts that April in 1977.

"Then I moved here, to Kansas City. When I got here, Stan – my future husband – was the faculty advisor for a brand-new Zen meditation group. He had never studied with anyone, but he was interested, he was faculty, and they needed an advisor. I don't know why they needed an advisor because there were no students in it. There was a guy who had sat a few sesshins with Eido Roshi[36]

---

34 Also known as Insight Meditation, a Theravadan practice.

35 The Precepts are commitments people taking up the Buddhist path agree to abide by. There are various levels depending upon one's degree of involvement. Judy tells me that in the Kwan Um School, "We have five precepts, ten precepts, sixteen precepts. And then forty-eight for people who really want more precepts." See Appendix 1.

36 Eido Shimano, a controversial Rinzai teacher who founded Dai Bosatsu Zendo Kongo-ji in the Catskill Mountains.

and a guy who had studied with Kobun Chino Otogawa,[37] there was me who'd studied with Zen Master Seung Sahn, there were a couple of other people who had studied with a couple of other teachers. We'd meet together and sort of try to figure out what form we wanted to use and what chants we wanted to use and stuff like that.

"Then Stan and I decided to get married. And I asked Zen Master Seung Sahn, I said, 'Oh, I'm going to get married. Can you perform the wedding?' And he said, 'How close is Chicago?' And I said, 'Oh, about an hour and a half.' Meaning by plane. And he thought I meant by car, and he said, 'Okay.' So he came out, and none of the other people's teachers came out, so that's how we became a Kwan Um Zen Center. Because he was the only teacher who came out. And he came out every year for something like a dozen years which is kind of amazing. It's a tiny town, not many people, but he would come out because we were sincere."

Roger Brennan[38]

Despite Meido Moore's reservation, not all Zen practitioners – not even all authorized Zen teachers – necessarily consider themselves Buddhist. A small but interesting group, for example, self-identify as Roman Catholic. Koun Yamada, fearing the demise of Zen in Japan, speculated that the Catholic church with its monastic traditions might provide a home for the practice. Many Catholic religious – both priests and nuns – studied with him, and he gave Dharma Transmission to seven, including Elaine MacInnes,[39] the first Canadian to be authorized to teach Zen. He told them that he had no intention of converting them to Buddhism but that he believed Zen could make them better Christians.

Roger Brennan is a priest in the Scarboro Mission Society who studied with Sister Elaine when they were both posted to the Philippines. When I met him, he was a member of the Oak Tree in the Garden Sangha in Toronto, headed by Patrick Gallagher,[40] who also worked with Sister Elaine.

"I grew up in a typical Catholic ambiance. Went to Catholic schools; had nuns for teachers. So we got a lot of stories of the saints and even as a very young person, I was intrigued by these. And although I wouldn't have known to describe it in this way at that time, I would say the mystics particularly

---

37 A Soto priest who came from Japan at the request of Shunryu Suzuki to assist him at Tassajara.

38 Modified from *Catholicism and Zen*, Sumeru: 2016, pp. 185-87.

39 Cf. *Zen Conversations*, pp. 73; 171.

40 Cf. *Zen Conversations*, p. 132.

intrigued me, that people could have these experiences. Growing up, I can remember that there was this curiosity, but when I went to Jesuit high school, I never really took to Jesuit spirituality, the Ignatian exercises. We certainly got them," he says with a chuckle. "But it never clicked with me. It was just not my spirituality. Then in the novitiate we studied this book by a priest named Adolphe Tanqueray. It was quite a thick book; it was considered a classic in mystical theology at that time. It gave a very, very detailed analysis of the road to perfection, and I kind of realized I was not on that road and figured I was never going to get on that road. It was not a very appealing road. It seemed to be something for people who were somehow extraordinary. It wasn't me at any rate. And that kind of allowed me to let go of that type of spirituality. It was something I couldn't do and didn't particularly want to do. So I just said my prayers and received the sacraments, and that was sort of it."

His first posting was to the Philippines. "I was assigned to a parish, but it was not a parish like we have here in Toronto. I think it covered something like a hundred square miles. There were thirty-five villages and one road, and that was the road along the coast, and the villages were mostly up in the mountains. So it was a matter of driving as far as you could and walking the rest of the way. It was a heavily sacramental ministry, marriages, baptisms, funerals, masses, that sort of stuff. Although what we tried to do was to bring all that down. Like, we wouldn't have mass every day. We would only do marriages at a certain time, and everybody had to get married together. So we were not just sacramental machines. Running a sacramental outlet was not what we were there for. We were there to build the church or assist in building the church, and, of course, it was obvious that the future of the church was in the lay people. So we decided we would minimize the sacramental work we did and put our energy into training lay leaders."

"Community leadership? Political leadership? Religious leadership?" I ask.

"Well, you know, it was everything. But we would start with social analysis, looking around. You know, you have a village of about fifty families, and they're absolutely destitute. So we'd begin by saying, 'Do you think this is the way God wants you to be? Your children dying, and you're hungry, and you know ...' So we'd work on that and try to help them come to the realization that that is not the God we worship. And then we would say, 'Well, why are you poor? What's going on?' And try to do a bit of social analysis in terms of why the situation was the way it was, and then bring in the religious dimension. 'Do you think this is the way God wants things to be?"

Then in the mid-'70s, his superiors called him back to Canada to do a course of study on scripture. "And I was not interested. I mean absolutely I was interested in scripture. But I was not interested in studying or teaching, which is what it would have become. I loved teaching, but I was not interested in teaching in the seminary. I loved what we were doing in the Philippines."

He was sent to St. Paul's University in Ottawa. One spring day he was in the library. "Ottawa can be beautiful in the spring, and it was one of those days when you would really like to be anywhere but in a library, and I would have given anything to be anywhere else but in that stack room. And I was just flipping through the books looking for the one I wanted and came across this thing a little bigger than a pamphlet on Eastern religions. And because it had nothing to do with scripture, I picked it up and just started flipping through it, looking at the index, looking to see what was in there. I can't even remember if it was about Buddhism in general or Zen. I suspect it might have been on Zen. And I started reading it. Well, then I forgot about the book I was looking for. I took the book and sat down and read through it. And it reawakened in me all the interest I had had years before with the saints and the mystics and that sort of thing. It looked at that reality or that possibility from a completely different perspective. It was no longer something for extraordinary people in certain circumstances. *This* was saying, 'You can experience the transcendent. Anybody can. You don't have to be a special kind of person.'

"So that really tweaked me; however, I still had to get my paper finished. So I put it back. Got the scripture book, finished my paper, decided not to continue, and got permission to go back to the Philippines. In the meantime, I was talking with some of Our Lady's Missionary sisters that I worked with, and I was telling them I was going back to the Philippines. And they said, 'Oh, isn't that great. One of our sisters who's been in Japan for years and has been studying Zen has been assigned not just to the Philippines but to Hinunangan,' which is the town that I was working in."

The sister was Elaine MacInnes, and, in Hinunangan, she introduced Roger to formal Zen practice. Shortly after this, she moved to Manila, where he occasionally went to attend sesshin. Following this initial training, however, he didn't have direct access to a Zen teacher for long periods of time and had to practice on his own, although he made use of sabbaticals to do brief stays with Koun Yamada in Japan.

"I'd say most of my life doing Zen, I've been somewhere where there wasn't a teacher."

"Why did you continue it?" I ask.

"Oh, because that simply became for me the way to pray."

I ask him to explain Zen to me as if I were unfamiliar with the practice, something, he tells me, he has done for other people on several occasions.

"I explain that first of all it is a way of meditating, a way of keeping your mind still. Sister Elaine used to give this description. She talks about the discursive mind, how one thought just follows on another and another and another, and that's something everyone can understand from experience. And she describes it as like being out on a lake on a day when it's windy and the water's stirred up, and you're in a boat and you look into the lake, you don't see anything. It's just all distorted. But if you go out on a lake, and the lake is perfectly smooth and you look down, you can see way into the depths of the lake. And so I tell people that it's kind of like that. You want to stop this discursive thinking because your mind is all muddy with all this stuff running through it.

"So the first thing you want to do is kind of stop all that and just be and let the mind be still and clear and look deeply into your own depths." The technique he introduces people to in order to do that is breath meditation. I ask if one couldn't accomplish the same end by a more traditional Christian practice.

"Well, that's the problem that drew me to Zen because – especially when I began to do Zen – we had learned lots of stuff about meditation but never learned *how* to do it. There was never a methodology, except perhaps the Jesuit Spiritual exercises, the Ignatian Exercises, but they turned me off."

I mention that Sister Elaine had told me something similar. That she had been drawn to the idea of contemplative prayer but hadn't been able to find anyone to show her how to do it until she took up Zen practice.

"So, I'm wondering if this is one of the things Zen can offer Catholics," I say, "a way back to contemplative prayer?"

"I certainly would say that. But – you know – the thing that amazed me when Sister Elaine came to Toronto and opened the zendo here, I thought she would be flooded with priests and religious. And I think over the years – fifteen years since she's been here – I think maybe two nuns, and a deacon and maybe one priest have ever shown any interest at all. And none of them stayed more than a short time. I'm not sure if Catholics are interested." He laughs. "Maybe it's only strange people who are interested."

2
Is Zen Unique?

All schools of Zen trace their origin back to a series of ancestors – sometimes called "Patriarchs" – who over the course of six generations melded Indian Buddhism with Daoism to create a uniquely Chinese sect. In the 6th century Chan spread to Vietnam where it is called Thien, in the 7th to Korea (Son), and not until the 12th to Japan (Zen), from where it eventually crossed the Pacific to North America in the early 20th century.

The new teaching had a profound social impact on the countries, particularly Japan, in which it arrived, but it was not the most common form of Buddhism in any of these lands. In Japan, the most numerous Buddhist sects remain the Jodo and Nichiren. In North America, less than 1.5 percent of the population self-identifies as Buddhist, the majority of whom are associated with ethnic communities similar to the congregation at Sokoji in San Francisco when Shunryu Suzuki was sent there. Tibetan, Vipassana, and secular mindfulness groups can be found as easily in most North American cities as Zen centers.

People with an interest in either Buddhism or meditation have options.

Seiso Paul Cooper

Seiso Paul Cooper began his Zen study with the Rinzai teacher Eido Shimano and completed his training with Sojun Diane Martin, founder of the Soto Udumbara Buddhist Training Institute in Illinois. He is a practicing psychoanalyst as well as a Zen teacher in Montpelier, Vermont. We met through Skype at the height of the pandemic when tight restrictions were in place throughout North America. Seiso admitted that he hadn't found them particularly difficult. I ask if he believes people with Zen experience were better prepared to deal with the situation than others might be.

"Well, I think of the Buddha's Three Marks of Existence," he tells me. "Emptiness, no self – no permanently existing self – and suffering. If we really have an experiential understanding of those factors it takes the edge off things. I think what the current situation's done to people is it's created an enormous amount of uncertainty. But uncertainty has always been a fact of life, and the illusion of certainty just got stripped away. In that regard, a Zen practitioner – or a Zen student who takes practice seriously – is going to be better equipped to deal with the reality of uncertainty because we knew about it already. I think that much of the panic that we're seeing is related to people who were not prepared in that way."

"The Three Marks of Existence is something recognized by all Buddhists," I point out. "Is there something that distinguishes Zen from other forms of Buddhism?"

"I think the underlying assumption and goal within the Mahayana tradition is the same regardless of the cultural overlays. I would say there are certain fundamental differences between – say – the Theravada traditions and the Mahayana traditions. And there's fundamental differences between the Rinzai and the Soto tradition within Zen."

"But aside from those internal differences, is there anything that distinguishes Zen in general from other forms of Mahayana Buddhism?"

"Well, again, Zen is a Mahayana tradition, and the underlying theme is, 'I vow to save all beings.' That means I'm going to stay on the wheel of life and death – samsara – and stick around. And the Theravada tradition, the idea is to get off the wheel. And then there's the distinction of realizing emptiness of the self in that tradition and recognizing the emptiness of all phenomena in Mahayana traditions."

"So there's no significant difference between Zen and – say – Tibetan Buddhism? Both of which are Mahayana?"

"In that sense I would say, 'No, they're not different.' But the cultural trappings are different. You know, in Tibetan Buddhism they have this idea that people come back as reincarnated lamas and stuff like that. My understanding is when you're dead, you're dead for a long time. That might not be an accurate interpretation of Zen Buddhism, but that's my understanding. And if there's any idea of returning or reincarnation or something like that, it is free of ego. So, you're dead, and your body rots away and goes into the Earth and the sky and everything else atomically or molecularly, if you will, and seeds new life. And we're all part of the interdependence of all. To me, it kind of looks like that."

Karin Kempe

Karin Kempe and Peggy Sheehan are the spiritual directors of the Zen Center of Denver. When Karin was studying at the Rhode Island School of Design, she "convinced the college that going to the Rochester Zen Center would be a good part of my development as an artist. So I went there to do a training period." It proved to be a good fit, and, after graduation, she moved to Rochester, although – like John Pulleyn – she was not a resident.

"I had found my path, and I was determined. It was a very intensive practice. There were about three hundred people in the community, living in houses very close to the center, and we'd go early in the morning to sit. We'd go every evening to sit. And then we'd often sit during the day. Many of us were sitting four to six hours a day and going to multiple sesshin a year."

Karin cleaned houses to earn money. When she realized that that was not going to be an adequate way to support herself, she received help from her family to study medicine. While in medical school she passed her first koan, married, and became a mother. After completing her residency, she and her family – after a short stint in Northern Florida – moved back to Denver. She continued her Zen practice while pursuing a medical career and eventually received Dharma transmission from both Danan Henry, a Kapleau heir, and then later Shishin Wick, a Dharma heir of Taizan Maezumi.[41]

"At heart, the various forms of Buddhism are all the same, the underlying insight is the same, and it is not even Buddhist. I think the fundamental insight is found in the Advaita[42] and in mystical Christianity and other traditions. The Zen path in particular is a pretty direct non-dual path, and then there is a lot of surrounding cultural and artistic expression that I find wonderful and inspiring and creative. But fundamentally I don't see a difference. An excellent Vipassana teacher, an excellent Tibetan teacher, a Dzogchen teacher, I would imagine we would essentially be saying the same thing."

She does admit, however, that Zen is more explicit in talking about awakening than some other traditions. "People have those experiences with these other paths, but Zen is pretty explicit despite – how should I put it? – the way we try to be careful about our language. We say there is 'nothing to attain,' but this non-attainment is a real experience. A lot of people come because they want what they call 'peace of mind,' they just want to not be turbulent inside and want to settle the discomfort of their active minds. That is a good reason to practice. But there are clearly also people who come to Zen because they know that there is something that they have not realized, and they want to realize it. That's their *Bodhicitta* leading them. And Zen is one of the practices that provides a path for that."

---

41   Maezumi was a Japanese born teacher who had transmission in the Soto, Rinzai, and Sanbo Zen lineages.

42   A Hindu spiritual discipline.

Kate Hartland

Kate Hartland is the guiding teacher of the Bright Sea Zen Sangha in North Weymouth, Massachusetts. She is also a member of a collective of New England Zen teachers who refer to themselves as the Dharma Wheel Asanga. When I speak to people in that group, they often mention the unique cultural elements of Japanese Zen. The style, as Kate points out, "is very pared down.

"Devotional aspects are very minimal in the way that they are expressed. There is a great emphasis on zazen, just sitting down on a cushion with some guidance and some prodding here and there but just sitting down on a cushion. And there's this great faith that one can awaken to one's true nature. Right? Very spare. Very simple. Very straightforward. It doesn't require any beliefs, doesn't require any particular devotional actions. Just look for yourself."

Meido Moore

"Buddhism is Buddhism," Meido Moore states in his forthright manner. "And Zen is a Mahayana tradition. It is also what we call an expression of the Ekayana, the One Vehicle. So it has a particular orientation that we can trace through the sutras, an approach to and an understanding of the Buddha's teachings. But if I had to say what distinguishes Zen, I would return always to the four lines attributed to Bodhidharma[43] – the great master who transmitted Zen to China – that describe it: 'A separate transmission outside the scriptures; not dependent upon – or setting up – words or letters;' and, crucially, the last two lines, 'directly pointing at the human mind; seeing one's nature, becoming Buddha.' Those four lines sketch out the approach and the method of Zen. And the method of Zen is summed up by those last two lines: it is a path in which the direct pointing activity of the teacher is intended – rapidly, at the beginning of the path – to cause us to have this recognition of our true nature, kensho. That is the gateway to the path. And then, taking that recognition as the basis of all subsequent practice, there is the maturation, the post-awakening path of progressive transcendence that we call 'becoming Buddha.' So, to see one's true nature; to become Buddha through directly pointing at the human mind: if I have to sum up the Zen approach in the most pithy way, that's it. Zen is not the only Buddhist path that has this kind of direct approach or that is dependent

---

43 A special transmission outside the scriptures;
    Not dependent on words or letters;
    By direct pointing to the mind of man,
    Seeing into one's true nature and attaining Buddhahood.

upon the activity of the teacher in such a manner, but I have to say that is the Zen way. That is what distinguishes it."

Hogen Bays

Hogen and Chozen Bays are the founders and co-abbots of Great Vow Monastery, a residential Zen community in Oregon. They have also worked with and welcomed teachers from other traditions. "I am interested in keeping my eye on the essence of practice," Hogen tells me. "So we have had many Buddhist teachers come here, such as Ajahn Amaro from the Theravadan school and several Vajrayana teachers with a Dzogchen[44] perspective and others. In recent years I've worked with Byron Katie.[45] My Zen practice has been quite rich, quite wide, looking at the truths of life from many different perspectives."

There is an element of free association in the way Hogen responds to questions. It's something he's aware of. "You have to forgive me, Rick. You ask these questions, and I can just go on a roll, as you can hear." I'm happy to let him roll on.

"Is there something in your experience that distinguishes Zen from these other forms of practice?" I ask.

"Well, I think that's exactly it. It's experience. If you're involved with the Theravada or Vajrayana[46] or some other forms of Buddhism, they often first require intellectual understanding, a cognitive understanding of the Path. This is fine. But, in Zen, scholarly understanding is secondary. For example, often in the Vajrayana tradition the teachings go through layer after layer of, 'This means this, that means this, this means that, therefore, therefore, therefore.' So when I read the teachings of Tsongkhapa or Kalu Rinpoche,[47] they appear to divide Buddhism up like the early Indian texts do. They describe Dharma as a granularized teaching. Modern Zen – or at least the Zen I'm familiar with – does not do that. It just asks, 'What is at the root?' The mind can endlessly think and particularize things, but what is at the heart of the matter? How can you step into that? Emphasizing what is before words does not make Zen special – because fundamentally everything begins before words – but in Zen Buddhism there is an emphasis on recognizing the truth before words, before

---

44   Dzogchen is the form of Tibetan Buddhist practice also known as the Great Perfection.

45   A non-affiliated spiritual instructor.

46   Tibetan Buddhism viewed as a third stream of Buddhism alongside the Theravadan (Hinayana) and the Mahayana.

47   Tsongkhapa was a 14th century Tibetan Buddhist teacher; Kalu Rinpoche is a contemporary Tibetan teacher.

differentiation. This is important. And this insight can be embodied. It can be lived.

"Koans are a unique tool for this investigation. A koan requires a total body/mind experience. It's not a thought process. They must be answered from the Oneness at the root of life. In the same way, one's spiritual practice has to be embodied in the entirety of one's life. It has to infuse your conversation; it has to penetrate your dreams; it has to come from the heart's essence. That heart essence functions through kindness, respect, total presence, and complete willingness to engage with circumstances as they arise for the benefit of as many people as possible.

"So, from the perspective of the heart's core, everyone is doing just fine. At the core there is a vibrant life-energy which comes out of nowhere, which is the creative juice of the universe, which each of us touches and embodies, which is not self-centered. A mature practice is not infused with getting. Of course, we all start that way, practicing because we want to know the Buddha-Mind, the Essence, the Truth. This boils down to a simple, 'I want, I want' and right there is a great big separate 'I.' As a practitioner ripens their emphasis is more on what they have, here, now.

"In my limited experience, the nature of mind is inclusive. It includes that 'I' and recognizes that it is a miracle and at the same time not special. Other traditions tend to say, 'I want to improve, polish, I want to make this, I want to become great, I want to become someone else, I want to become the Dalai Lama, I want to become Thich Nhat Hanh.' This attitude of 'getting better' of gaining is a particular orientation of practice common to many traditions, but anything we get we can also lose. Recognizing the steadfast core – the transcendent, the inclusive, the one bright mind, the heart of the matter – is to see fundamentally that the universe is not broken; it's not divided into good and evil; it's one inclusive whole. That – I think – is a unique Zen Buddhist understanding of the Dharma.

"So, in Zen we emphasize directly experiencing that which is immanent, inclusively present. In some Buddhist texts, this direct knowing is something described as taking hundreds of thousands of lifetimes to realize. Practice for infinite lives, and then you'll become Buddha. But in the Zen tradition – and experientially – right here, in this moment, the inclusive nature of mind is fully developed. You can touch that. You can recognize that. And while I think that's a truth recognized in other Buddhist traditions, it's much more alive in the Zen tradition. This is the non-cognitive expression of the Dharma. And, of course, even if we awaken right now, it will take us lifetimes to learn to embody it and live skillfully."

Is Zen Unique?

Dosho Port

Dosho Port[48] and his wife, Tetsugan Zummach,[49] maintain the Vine of Obstacles website, an online support program for Zen training. He puts the matter in a historical perspective.

"I think what distinguishes Zen – not that it's necessarily practiced this way now – is that it's a path that insists that you can wake up in this lifetime and do the kind of post-awakening process that's necessary to live compassionately to benefit all beings.

"What happened when Buddhism was introduced into China is that there was an influx of Mahayana texts which described a series of stages before complete enlightenment. A number of the systems describe fifty-two stages, although they're not necessarily the same stages. Then at least by the time of Mazu,[50] the Chinese Chan masters were just cutting through it all. They were teaching sudden awakening in this life. 'This very mind is Buddha.' And I think those two – the sudden and the gradual – became two foci: sudden awakening and a gradual post-awakening process. So then the methods they developed to help people catalyze that which they already are is what characterizes the Zen tradition. And the key ingredient is a whole-heartedness and one-doing-ness – just throwing yourself into it – that is present throughout the tradition and, for practitioners, is the heart of the matter. Just throwing yourself into it. And I think the Japanese did really well at maintaining that and developing it."

"It?" I ask.

"The path to kensho and post-kensho training. There are parallels in other systems, but the practice methods are unique to Zen. For example, the koan and the keyword method.[51] I don't think that other schools have harnessed the power of Dharma narrative in the same way that the Zen tradition has, using Dharma narrative to break through all narrative and tell a story about it. Hakuin Zenji[52] in the 18th century and his successors have probably made the greatest contributions to the post-awakening process in all of Buddhist history."

---

48 Cf. *Zen Conversations*, pp. 71; 90-91.

49 Cf. *Zen Conversations*, pp. 64-65.

50 Mazu Daoyi, an 8th century Chan master famed for his "strange words and extraordinary actions." He is reputed to have had 139 Dharma heirs.

51 A "key word" is a single word or phrase taken from a koan which becomes the focus of one's meditation.

52 18th century Japanese Rinzai master who revised the koan system.

Cynthia Kear

"First and foremost, what distinguishes Zen is zazen, sitting meditation," Cynthia Kear tells me. "This is the primary path/vehicle/gate through which we come to greater wisdom and compassion." *Prajna*/wisdom and *karuna*/compassion are the traditional goals of Zen practice. "So there's a tremendous emphasis on just sitting and a trust that if we come into stillness and awareness we will transform a lot of suffering and get in touch with our own inherent Buddha Nature.

"I also think that there is a strong emphasis on the Precepts. I was just reading an excerpt from one of Suzuki Roshi's early Dharma talks about wisdom and the importance of Precepts, and Precepts as a way to bring ourselves into alignment with our Buddha Nature. These are my words, so not quoting directly. So I think Zen practice is also about entering into a vow-based life where we really want to uphold the Precepts, where they're really prominent."

"Isn't that much the same with other forms of Buddhism?" I ask.

"Maybe not to the same degree. I don't know, but I know this is part of Suzuki Roshi's lineage."

"What about enlightenment or awakening? Are those terms you use?"

"Very, very judiciously. I think with the influence of Dogen and his direction, it's less about awakening and enlightenment as being something that's out there that we have to work for, but more about practice realization. If I am here with you – fully connected heart and mind – then this is practice realization. This is it. And it's not something that highfalutin or out of our reach. This is really key, to be really present with what we are doing every moment. So I think 'awakening' and 'enlightenment' are very judiciously used. It's more about transforming suffering."

Scott Thornton

"To me, Zen is different from general Buddhism in a fundamental sense in that there really isn't any requirement as a Zen practitioner to even be a Buddhist," Scott Thornton says. "I know plenty of people who are not. And I know a lot of people who say, 'Yeah. I'm Buddhist. But I'm also Christian, or I'm also atheist.' I've known a lot of people who refer to themselves as a JewBu because they practice both Judaism and Buddhism."

"Not all of them are Zen practitioners though," I say. "Is there something that distinguishes Zen from other Mahayana practices?"

"I'm not really so scholarly about this, but I would say that Sanbo Zen and Rinzai Zen, those two specifically really focus on awakening, and they focus on koans to help achieve that awakening. But, you know, lately Henry Shukman has been emphasizing that it's okay even for a Sanbo Zen student of thirty years not to have had an awakening. He recently gave an example of a woman he read about, I think in one of Jack Kornfield's[53] books. He had examples of some people who had had experiences, and there was one woman who had been a teacher – I think a Soto teacher – for thirty years and had never had a big experience. And yet she came to realize that she was fundamentally different than she had been thirty years prior. And people would tell her, 'You're more yourself. You're kinder. You're wiser.' And she really seemed to see the world in an enlightened way, just couldn't point to some experience and say that's where it started."

Sarah Bender

Sarah Bender is the resident teacher of the Springs Mountain Sangha in Colorado Springs. She began her Zen study in 1979 in Honolulu with Robert Aitken. Later, when she moved to Colorado, she sat with a couple of other teachers while her children were small and attended a few retreats with Thich Nhat Hanh and the Catholic Zen teacher, Pat Hawk. She met Joan Sutherland[54] – a John Tarrant heir from whom Sarah would eventually receive transmission – when Father Hawk was unable to facilitate a scheduled retreat because of health reasons. "He suggested that I call John Tarrant, and John said, 'I can't come, but I have this brand-new teacher, Joan Sutherland. Give her a call.'" Joan agreed to lead the retreat, assisted by David Weinstein who served as Head of Practice.

"I think what first really drew me to Zen was its radical simplicity," Sarah reflects. "You know, sit down, shut up, and see what happens. And its sort of deconstructive nature. Really you were not this, not this, not this, and then see what is. And just sitting. You know? I'm very much a language person, and the beauty of koan language drew me immediately. There was just a resonance there. But Buddhist teachings with the eight this's and the twelve that's didn't pull me in the same way."

"In that case," I ask, "how important are the 'eight this's' and 'twelve that's'? How important is the Buddhist matrix to Zen? Can one practice Zen without it?"

"A number of Zen teachers I know, including Joan, have said at times that they wouldn't call themselves Buddhist. But Joan, for example, is a brilliant

---

53   An American Vipassana teacher and popular writer.

54   Cf. *Zen Conversations* pp. 41-42;49-50; 84-85; 110-11; 128-32; 161-62.

Buddhist scholar and translator. It's just that that's not all she is."

"And the whole thing about Bodhidharma's 'special transmission outside the scriptures, not dependent on words and letters?'" I ask.

"Well, that has nothing to do with not learning it. You know, all the people who were saying that were people who were extremely, deeply versed in the tradition. What they were saying is that *just* the words and letters won't do it. Transmission is not a matter of words and letters."

"What is it a matter of then?"

"In my experience, it's a matter of the thing that appears – the thing that arises – when two people together encounter the Great Matter of Life and Death with minds that are able to fall open in the same time and place. So the experience of one is not identical to the other, but it is a core experience that's transformative. So it's not like, 'I've got this; I give it to you' exactly. It's, 'I've got this, and I can help you.'"

Winifred Shokai Martin

Winifred Shokai Martin is Dublin-born and there is still an Irish lilt to her speech. She is an ordained priest at the Buddhist Temple of Toledo established by Rinsen and Do'on Weik.[55] Her first exposure to Buddhist practice, however, had been a Vipassana course she took while working in administration at Eastern Michigan University. "It's a public university and understaffed, and I guess Human Resources felt that support staff were stressed, which was probably true, and they offered a six-week course in meditation. It was very secular and cognitively oriented. And I did that six-week course and felt an instant connection with it."

After the course ended, Shokai sat for a while with a Vipassana group in Ann Arbor, fifty miles from Toledo. "It was pretty secular for the most part, but I felt like I was being drawn further and further in."

When she saw an article in the newspaper about the Zen group established by Rinsen and Do'on in Toledo, she thought, "'Oh, well, Ann Arbor's an hour away. I might as well go and hang out with these Zen people.' Knew nothing about Zen, absolutely nothing. So it was a Wednesday night. And it wasn't a temple at that stage, it was just a Zen Center. But they did have liturgy. So I walked into liturgy, which triggered all of my Catholic hang-ups. I was not anticipating this, because the Vipassana group had nothing to do with ritual or liturgy. But I still felt an instant alignment with it. I remember that first night there was an older woman who kind of looked out for me. And even though

---

55 Rinsen Weik, cf. *Zen Conversations*, Pp. 51-52; 80-83; 111-15;132-34.

here I was in the middle of liturgy thinking, 'Oh! What am I doing?' she just guided me through it in such a beautiful, compassionate way. She could see that I was on the edge of, 'Oh, I'm just gonna leave.' I think it was a combination of this and meeting that compassionate heart in action in the heart of bowing! You know, I'd never bowed before in my life! There was just something in that combination that just opened things up even more for me."

I ask if she thought there were a significant difference between Vipassana and Zen practice.

"So both shikan taza and Vipassana are choiceless awareness practices. I think for me in Vipassana, at least in the beginning – and I only practiced it for a year or maybe eighteen months – you're kind of waiting for something to arise. You're noting as things arise. Whereas in shikan taza, you're not doing that; it's just open awareness. So that's a subtle difference. I think probably the deeper you go into both of them, the more they merge."

"That's a distinction between two meditation techniques," I point out. "But as a path, as an expression of Dharma, as a practice as a whole, is there much difference between the two?"

"I would be supremely happy with both. For me, Vipassana was the gateway. So for myself, can I say what I do now is significantly different? I can't."

A moment later, however, she does think of one difference. Personal interviews with the teacher – called dokusan or sanzen – are a central element of Zen practice. "So there are superficial differences," she says.

"Do you consider that a superficial difference?" I ask.

"Well, I think Zen is very much mind to mind. You know, we do dokusan. If I have a question about my meditation practice, I would speak to my teacher directly. Vipassana, lots of group instruction and exploration."

Jeff Shore

Jeff Shore is professor emeritus of Zen Studies at the Rinzai-affiliated Hanazono University in Kyoto, where he taught for 34 years. After 25 years of practice at the Tofukuji training monastery in Kyoto, he became the first Westerner to complete the Rinzai koan training in Japan under a Japanese Zen master.

Jeff explains that formal Zen training in Japan is arduous, and many of the students at the university are bewildered by why Americans and Europeans have any interest in it. Many of his students are the sons of priests who will inherit their father's temple. For these young men, "It's a very different system. They may not want to be a priest, but they have to be. And then here's people like us coming halfway around the world. We're not even going to become priests;

we're not going to have a temple. And yet we're putting ourselves through this. They wonder why? So that's how I try to interest the students."

"You're teaching Japanese students how westerners see Zen?" I ask.

"More or less, yes. What do we see that they don't?"

He's careful in responding to my question about what distinguishes Zen from other forms of Buddhism, speaking slowly and reflectively, "I would say that Zen offers a direct method, and it doesn't get too bogged down in ritual or even meditation. Meditation doesn't become something that can actually prevent you from going on in your practice. Most important, I would say, doubt itself. In Zen you should have doubt – genuine doubt – which actually becomes a tool of the practice. So rather than pushing away your doubt and telling someone to have faith, for example, doubt becomes a tool in the practice. I think this is very relevant for people in the 21st century. Because who do you know who doesn't have doubt? Of course, to make that into a real spiritual doubt is another thing. But to begin with, it is already there. So rather than pooh-pooh the doubt, Zen says, 'You have doubt? Good. Take that doubt all the way.' This is one of the strong points of real Zen practice."[56]

I ask what he means by saying that meditation shouldn't become something that gets in the way of practice.

"Well, a lot of so-called Zen practice is actually a form of ritual, including meditation, sitting in a certain posture, having a certain mind-set for a certain period of time. When you look at it really critically, people who do that are actually avoiding the real practice. They're escaping although they may be sitting in zazen posture. In other words, a person may be struggling with something and so they seek out a meditation teacher – perhaps a Zen teacher – and they learn how to sit in a certain way. They learn how to focus their mind on something, and it's like a drug. It allows them to get away from the thing that is hurting them. So it can actually become, literally, like a drug, an escape from the thing they're suffering. The whole point, I would say, of Zen practice is not to do that, but actually – instead of trying to get *out* of it – to go all the way *in*, 'cause that's the only way to get out of it."

"Is that why Zen stresses the importance of working with a teacher?" I ask.

"Well, not absolutely. If you look at the life of Gautama Buddha, it's a prime example of someone who didn't have a teacher. But it's certainly helpful to have a guide who's gone through it, although a teacher can become an escape too."

---

56   Cf. Jeff's translation of the 17th century *Great Doubt: Practicing Zen in the World* by the Chinese Chan teacher Boshan (Wuyi Yuanlai). Wisdom Publications, 2016.

3

WHAT DO ZEN TEACHERS TEACH?

James Ford

James Ford is a central figure in the establishment of contemporary Zen in North America. He trained and received transmission in both the Soto School, through Jiyu Kennett,[57] and the Harada-Yasutani lineage through John Tarrant. He co-founded and was the first abbot of the Boundless Way Zen collective in New England and later established the Empty Moon Zen Network on the West Coast. His Dharma heirs include some of the most recognized and respected teachers in the United States, people like Melissa Blacker[58] of the Worcester Boundless Way Temple, Rinsen Weik, and Dosho Port, with whom I have worked since the death of Albert Low.[59] That makes James one of the ancestors acknowledged in the lineage chant of the school in which I practice.

"The primary function of the Zen path and, therefore, the task of the Zen teacher, is the project of awakening. And awakening, I believe, is a relatively narrowly defined thing. It is our direct, visceral insight into our wild openness, its manifestation within and as interdependence, and its expression in each little temporary thing that arises including you and me."

"Which," I point out, "doesn't answer the question of what a Zen teacher teaches, because you can't teach awakening."

"Well, you can't. No. So the better teachers understand that. Although I do notice most authorized Zen teachers say they can. What Zen teachers really can teach are specific disciplines associated with awakening. Zazen, shikan taza, koan introspection."

I ask if it is important that teachers also be able to present the basics of Buddhist theory.

"It is an interesting question. I've noticed people who are authorized to teach often don't seem to know a lot about Buddhism. Sometimes that's okay because they have big hearts, and they have some taste of the intimate. Maybe

---

57 The British-born founder of Shasta Abbey in California.

58 Cf. *Zen Conversations*, pp. 38-39.

59 Cf. *Zen Conversations*, pp. 49; 70; 87; 123.

they can guide people with that and maybe not. But bottom line I do believe the Buddhadharma requires some – *some* – technical knowledge."

The question only comes up because what was originally a monastic practice – a practice undertaken in an environment where students were immersed in sutra study and devotional activity on a daily basis – has been taken up in North America and Europe largely by non-monastics.

"Normative Zen practice until Japan – and certainly this was true in China, Vietnam, Korea until the last hundred years or so – is a monastic discipline that is only lightly touched upon by householders. Then Japanese Zen opened up that potentiality which, only in Japan, takes itself toward a logical conclusion in the last several hundred years in that county. We inherited all of that here in North America and are still struggling with what it all means."

Among other things it means that people authorized to teach Zen in North America no longer need to be ordained or be monastically trained.

"I think the real problem in the institution of Zen at this point is that the purpose of the practice is associated with our awakening," James continues. "And our awakening is itself incomplete. Or, perhaps better, not enough. I've come to have this little slogan: 'There's waking up, and there's growing up.' And these two things need each other, but they're not the same project. A boatload of Zen in the West is unconcerned with the whole part of growing up. I think we've seen the consequences of that omission."

"'A boatload.' So, a large portion of the Zen community fails to take maturing as seriously as they should. Is that what you just said?"

"That is my view."

"We say that teachers have 'transmission.' What does that mean? What is 'transmitted'?"

"That's kind of a delightful question. In China, transmission was this thing. It had nothing to do with ordination. It was conferred upon monks, nuns, and householders. Monks and nuns tended to own the franchise, but there are dramatic historical examples that this 'thing' can happen with just about anyone. The rhetoric is grand. It speaks to the mind-to-mind transmission, the sense that there is something to apprehend. And people do apprehend it. So, I've come to believe that transmission is a signifier that somebody within a lineage has confidence that somebody else has some depth of insight and believes that individuals can share that with others. Clearly in reality people get transmission for all sorts of different reasons. But that remains the hope as I see it."

"Calling it 'mind-to-mind' transmission implies a sense of continuity, doesn't it?" I ask. "Which, of course, is what lineage chants attest. The Buddha passed it on to Mahakasyapa who passed it onto Ananda who conferred it to someone else who passed it on to Robert Aitken, who passed it on to John

Tarrant, who passed it on to James Ford. It implies a continuity of insight."

"It does. And it's a wonderful symbol, and I believe it points to some true things. And anybody who pays attention to the history of it knows that it's a blending of history and mythology. It used to be more important than it is in the moment. In my first twenty years on the Zen way, transmission was important if for no other reason than it sorted out frauds and poseurs and people who just wanted some kind of authority over other people. Now that there are so many people with transmission and the quality and the expectations of what you need to receive transmission has become so diffuse, we're back to square one. I think finding a teacher with some kind of formal transmission within lineage is a necessary but not sufficient condition for somebody who's aspiring to follow the Zen way for themselves. But that's just the first thing on a longer check list. That growing up part is also important, very important. To practice Zen deeply one needs to commit to a teacher. But not all teachers are worthy of that kind of trust. Keep an open heart but also keep an engaged brain."

Winifred Shokai Martin

"When you talk about Rinsen," I say to Shokai Martin, "the term you use is 'teacher.' You haven't called him your priest or your minister or your spiritual director. You say, 'He's my teacher.' So what does a Zen teacher teach?"

"Well, I guess that the standard answer is, 'What is there to teach? There are no teachers of Zen.'" She's referring to the 11th case in the *Blue Cliff Record*, in which Huangbo[60] says this to his students. When one then inquires, "What about all those who in many places lead followers, what do they do?" Huangbo answers, "I did not say there was no Zen, just no teachers of Zen."

"Why call him a 'teacher' then?" I ask.

"Oh, because I need to be taught," Shokai tells me, laughing.

"Ah, gee, you've been messin' around in the koans again, haven't you?"

"What can I say? They just mess with your mind."

"Okay, let's look at it this way. You've got a board of directors. So, what's the teacher's job description from their perspective? In case they ever have to hire a new one and have to put an ad in the paper."

"Well, the ad in the paper would say 'abbot.' But for the sangha, it's someone who works for the realization of everyone they meet. And those they don't meet."

"'Someone who works for the realization of everyone they meet.' What does that mean?"

---

60   Obaku in Japanese.

"It means you might not be the same person for two different people. You meet the mind of your student. And you allow your student – in the shoken[61] relationship – to have that relationship with you where you're both completely vulnerable to that."

"Okay. To what end?"

"To what end? To awakening. Which is awakening to wisdom and compassion. To realization. To just being who you really are. Just allowing that to happen."

"Is that at all different from what a psychologist does?"

"There are so many different traditions in psychology. I mean you could look at psychology as self-improvement. Zen is not self-improvement. And certainly there's an end-goal in a psychological service, so you can operate more skillfully in the world. And that's great; we're big fans of good psychology. But that's not going to bring you to awakening. It can certainly help you because you know yourself better. You've got to know all the nooks and crannies and all the dark stuff within yourself to do this work. So therapy can be great. I'm a big fan of therapy."

"Okay. So the teacher's responsibility is to help people to awaken to wisdom and compassion. I'm pretty sure I know what you mean by 'compassion.' What do you mean by 'wisdom'?"

"'Wisdom' is seeing into the nature of who you really are. Of what 'this' is."

"But in a different way than I'd do that with a psychologist."

"Yes. With a psychologist, you're in the system. You're in ... I want to use the word 'samsara,' but we're talking about psychology. You're in this system of habituation and personality and all of that stuff. With Zen, you are actually working outside of that system. And you can never come to realization within the system. It's like Einstein said, 'You can't solve the problems within the problem.'[62] So in Zen you make it all bigger. You don't deny or repress the system; you see it for what it is. And you are still very much in this body, in this personality, in this world."

"And does this actually affect the way I interact with other persons and the cultural and physical environments in which I live?"

"If it doesn't, it's not working. It's a total integration. Right here, sitting at this desk with the mad cat roamin' around. Right here, right now. It's not separate. It's not separate from it. And it *is* it."

"Not separate from what?"

---

61 Formal relationship between teacher and student.

62 Usually quoted as "We can't solve problems by using the same kind of thinking we used when we created them."

"From this realization. From this awakened mind."

Sarah Bender

Sarah Bender hesitates when I ask her what a Zen teacher teaches, so I rephrase the question. "Do people think of you as a teacher?"

"They do."

"And when they use that term, how do they understand the transactional relationship between you?"

"I ask myself that question often," she tells me with a chuckle. "'What do they think I'm teaching?'" We sit in silence for a while – it's a natural Zen thing to do – before she continues. "Mostly I'm providing a shared experience of awakening, I think. And I do sutra studies; I do koan studies. I provide the practice; I provide a companionship in the practice of koan meditation and meditation without koans as well. Not all my students are koan students. And – you know – there are occasions to hang out in the company of our ancestors, in the company of the stories of the koan way. And in the silences. So it feels to me as if rather than conveying …"

She stops speaking again for a while, then says, "I think my students would say I'm not that good at teaching, but that they love me as their teacher, and they're grateful to me for the guidance that I give them. So I don't know. I don't think it's that easy to define."

Rafe Martin

Rafe Martin was an early student and friend of Philip Kapleau. The lay community he leads, the Endless Path Zendo, is located just three blocks from the Rochester center. He tells me that when he was a young man, he took up Zen training to help cultivate the traditional goals of wisdom and compassion. I ask how he imagined it would do that.

"Well, we all have traditions of sitting quietly and paying attention. We might say that there is a basic human tradition of meditation, of paying attention, being present, noticing what arises in the mind and then of exploring how you then act upon it or live it. To my mind, Zen is one of the most, if not *the* most practical doorway to such awareness."

"What does that have to do with wisdom and compassion?"

"It seems that most of the problems in the world begin with self-centeredness. Look at Putin.[63] He thinks in order to be happy he has the right to murder

---

63 Our conversation took place during the 2022 Russian invasion of the Ukraine.

people and destroy a culture. Take away such overweening self-centeredness, and – who knows? – you might have a decent human being. Look at how we as a species are treating the environment, the Earth around us, other people. We seem to think we're entitled to do whatever pleases us no matter the harm it causes.

"But what is this 'self' that wants all this *stuff* and thinks it's entitled to have it? What if it's all just smoke and mirrors? What if we've gotten ourselves hypnotized into thinking this 'self' should be what's in the driver's seat? What if by doing zazen or meditating, we uncover a missing, deeper, more fundamental sense of connection with other people, with animals, trees, rivers, mountains, sun, moon, and stars. You find that you're already home, and don't need all that additional 'stuff.' You find that you can actually get along in this world in a happier way because, being less caught up in yourself, you feel more deeply in touch with everything. For instance, you're happier when you eat because, not lost in thoughts about what you have to do next, you actually taste your food. Or you're happier when you look at a flower because you *really* see it. Or you're happier because, when your child is crying you don't even think, 'Why'd they do that stupid thing?' – that is, you're not thinking about how it impacts or says something about you – but instead, you simply reach out and hold her. In other words, such happiness *is* wisdom, *is* compassion, and it's our birthright, a birthright we're typically cut off from by our self-centered, isolating, habitual, unconscious thoughts about me, myself, and I and about what that 'I' is supposed to have or be.

"So if I can see through even a little bit of that 'me,' and what *I'm* supposed to have and what I think *I'm* entitled to, maybe not only am I happier, but I treat the world better. It's no longer separate from me but *is* me. Which changes everything. To me, that's what zazen is about and what it offers. It's helping me see where I'm getting caught and shooting myself in the foot, making things tougher than they need to be. Which is all it comes down to."

"When you first went to Rochester in the '70s, most of the people coming there did so because they'd read *The Three Pillars* and were seeking 'enlightenment.'"

"Right. We all wanted 'enlightenment.' Only there is no such thing *you're* going to get ... Let me qualify that. It doesn't mean that there isn't enlightenment. It's just that *you* won't get 'enlightenment.' *You're* not going to be enlightened. Instead, the burdensome isolating idea of 'you' will fall away into a new/old intimacy with all things: people, trees, sun, moon, stars, dogs, cats, cracks in the sidewalk, garbage cans, ants, and worms. You find you're home. So *you* don't *get* enlightened. Rather, by focusing on the practice – the breath count, the experience of the breath, the koan – we lose that compulsive interest in ourselves, and an original intimacy with all things – which in reality has always been there – can come to the fore."

"So, what does a Zen teacher do?"

"Geez! Tough question ... Okay, from my perspective now, I can show people how to sit in zazen. I can help them not walk off a cliff or walk into traffic in what they do. That is, not make the same kind of grievous mistakes I'd initially made practicing without a teacher. And, if they're interested in practice-realization, which in our tradition would typically mean koan practice, I can try to make sure they're not remaining stuck with some conceptual response that they think they can carry around in their pocket. It has to be real. It has to be in their life without attachment to concept. From the ground of practice-realization, they have to personally actualize it. My job is to see if that's going on for real and not accept it if it's not.

"In a sense the teacher's job is to be a friend to someone's aspiration and try to help them actualize their deepest aims. At the core, because we're all in this together – we're all beginners – such aims tend to coalesce in the aspiration of the *Bodhisattva*.[64] Which is what Zen is about: the Way of the Bodhisattva.

"So what I try to do is convey to people that it's really about seeking to touch base with who you really are, not who you've convinced yourself or the world's convinced you to think you are. And then see what happens. I can't guarantee anything, but let's see what happens. Let's go into that. And the tradition is there – in my view – to help you do just that. And, you know, when we speak about awakening – which implies from a dream – it doesn't mean you denigrate the dream. The dream is *it*! Fully. Awakening is to realize where you've always been. You don't throw away the life you have. You learn to live where you are, as you are, and mature further from that ordinary ground. Opportunities are there every day to do that. And if anyone gets the feeling that somehow they're special, I also try to make sure that they realize that they're not."

Seiso Paul Cooper

"I think prajna – wisdom – is natural," Seiso muses. "It's our intuitive way of being in the world, but it gets pushed away because we are over-reliant on the intellect. Practice helps bring that perception into the foreground and pushes the intellectual discursive thinking into the background, or at least gets them into an equal place. My gripe with seeking prajna or kensho or anything like

---

64 An enlightened (*Bodhi*) being (*sattva*). Certain historic or legendary Bodhisattvas function much the same as saints in the Christian tradition. At the personal level, one who aspires to be a Bodhisattva vows to practice for the benefit of all "sentient beings." See Appendix 2.

that – and you've probably heard this before from Soto people – is that it's seeking a particular state of mind. And my understanding of Dogen's teachings is that Zen is about actions and relationships, not about a preferred state of mind.

"So I think my role as a Zen teacher is I'm like the pitstop guy in the Indianapolis 500. All the people in my sangha do incredible things. One person is the chair and director of a community program for seniors. Another person in the sangha is a librarian, and a lot of homeless people come into the library in bad weather 'cause it's open to the public, and so she interacts with them and finds ways of helping them out. And she's also organized a community garden to grow vegetables to distribute to people. My wife, Karen, has done a lot of training on dealing with sexual slavery and children who get kidnapped into that world. Another person teaches yoga and zazen in the local prison. So, I don't do anything. I'm just there to support them. Like the guy in the pitstop, I help them change their tires, their psychic tires. Help them stay motivated when they're feeling burnt out, disgusted, and frustrated. Get them to see how the teaching and practice could help them face problems, turn the problems into challenges. Nudge them in that direction."

Judy Roitman

"Beats me," Judy Roitman says with seeming frankness when I ask what a Zen teacher teaches.

"Seriously. So the Kwan Um School of Zen used to have this series of audio tapes – the guy who sponsored it left, so we don't have it anymore – but we used to have this series called, 'Sit/Breathe/Vow.' It was done by this guy who was one these Unitarian-Buddhist people, and he was living at the Cambridge Zen Center, but then he got a fulltime gig in Utah as a Unitarian minister so he was no longer available to do it. So it stopped. But he would ask that question, 'What do you teach?' And if I had an idea that this is what I teach, then it's like a horse with blinders. You can't see what's there, what people actually need. Now Zen Master Seung Sahn was famous for always saying, 'I don't teach Buddhism. I just teach, "Don't know."' And there's some truth in that. If you say" – she deepens her voice – "'This is my teaching. I teach that all things are one' or 'I teach emptiness,' then it's like you've limited yourself, and it also becomes cognitive. You have to use cognition, but cognition shouldn't run the show. And that's why when you ask, 'What does a Zen teacher teach?' I really mean it when I say, 'I have no idea!' And 'I have no idea' is actually a very good teaching."

Hogen Bays

"There is a story I like to tell about Yamada Mumon Roshi and my teacher, Shodo Harada, who was his disciple."[65] Hogen Bays and I are talking about the role of Zen priests and their distinctive way of dress which necessarily stands out more in places like rural Oregon than it would in, say, Seattle. "Mumon Roshi was ardently against war. And, after World War II, as an act of atonement, he travelled to places of violence offering ceremonies for all the war dead. One day when they were travelling together, Mumon Roshi saw a person in a military uniform. He said, 'Isn't that wonderful.' And Harada said, 'Why wonderful? That is a person dedicated to violence.' Mumon Roshi said, 'Yes, but this person really shows what they believe in. They are expressing their faith, and that – in this time and age – is very important.'

"I think it is vital that we are people of visible dedication. I think it is significant when people step forward and say, 'I am reliably confident in this path of Dharma. I wear my faith overtly.' As you know, in the traditional story about the Buddha encountering the four messengers,[66] the fourth messenger was an ordained priest, a spiritual seeker, a monk. That willingness to be recognized as one who points out that there is a path to awakening is an aspect of being a priest.

"So the role of the priest, monk, shaman, spiritual guide has historically been an integral part of every community. All groups of people have need for someone to facilitate those human rituals of birth, becoming an adult, illness, loss, and death. I think one of the functions of being a priest is to support people through these normal transitions, to help people celebrate important life events by bringing them into a larger context, to help hold a more inclusive view. Birth-and-death are not just personal matters; they are important to the whole of creation. As we mature from birth to death, we affect our whole community, and the consequences ripple out. Having someone help us recognize the place of these vital life transitions is another aspect of being a priest."

"Pastoral care," I suggest.

"Absolutely. That is another way of saying it. Pastoral care. I think there are three kinds of care: the rituals of caring, the rituals of holding, and actions of personal care. Here our ordained persons work like pastors in a congregation. So, if someone is sick in our sangha, we call them; we go to the hospital to visit

---

65 Both Yamada and Harada are common names. Yamada Mumon was a Rinzai teacher who lived from 1900 to 1988. Harada Shodo is the residing abbot of Sogenji in Okayama. He also maintains Tahoma Sogenji in Washington State.

66 The Buddha is said to have undertaken the spiritual path after seeing a sick person, an old person, a dead body, and a monk.

them; we help them with food. I think leaders need to keep the eye of a shepherd on the sangha. That's another role of a priest. Additionally, there are the roles of teaching and holding and embodying the Buddhadharma, taking care of the facilities and methods which support practice. These have been passed down, in some way or another, for decades and generations. Another role is the personal commitment and the anchoring of one's life in spiritual practice. Because if you're a priest, and you take it seriously, that becomes the *raison d'être*, that becomes the core that holds you to practice, so that you also become accountable to yourself."

"And what is it that you hope for the people who spend time in residence at Great Vow? What do you hope they get out of it?"

"There are many benefits to residential practice. Often they happen at the same time. One essential benefit of community living is recognizing that one is not broken, that one is doing just fine. Having someone in the community who recognizes the nature of mind, the nature of nature, and understands that each person who shows up is the culmination of an entire lifetime of experiences, who knows each person has done their very best each moment of their life. I remember standing in front of fifty types of olive oil and, with almost no information, still trying to choose the best. We all often approach life in this way. In every situation, we each endeavor to make the best choice among our options. So, on one hand, as a spiritual teacher, it is important to view each person as at the pinnacle of their life. The apex of hard, hard work over the course of many years, having done their best with the mind and skills they have. This view is very important to me, because with this view your relationship begins with respect and not with, 'This is a broken, needy person.' Rather here is a person who is whole and complete, lacking nothing. To live with people who can see your wholeness is a great benefit.

"The next benefit is learning to recognize that each of us has potential to see life more deeply, more clearly, to let go of some of the detritus and fog which interferes with a healthy life. As a practitioner's mind becomes clearer, their behavior will reflect the heart of compassion and the mind of incisive wisdom. As leaders, we must have an open view about each person's future. To think we know how their life should look is delusion because everybody knows how they see the world and what choices they think they have better than we do. Still, even in my ignorance, I always hope that people in residential training will learn to be more skillful, to open the heart of compassion, to see with the eye of wisdom, to make the best of their particular life.

"Third, there is an opportunity for someone to learn their particular way of offering the medicine of Dharma. I'm very happy to facilitate ordained and lay people wanting to become carriers of the Dharma."

"And what are the specific roles of a teacher on this path?" I ask.

"Anyone who finds themself in this position – talking as I'm talking now – must first really listen to what is coming out of their mouth and then live in accord with what they're teaching. Being in this role demands that we cultivate kindness, that we cultivate ethical living, that we cultivate the very qualities that we are espousing to other people. So as teachers we need to be continually looking into the nature of our own mind and refining our skills.

"Another aspect is that the Dharma teachings are both eminently simple and extremely rich. The Dharma is very deep and can be looked at from many different vantage points. To be able to see what is at the core of those different views and to try to organize them into a presentation that offers people a clear sense of the spiritual path – its purpose and direction – is another of responsibility of a teacher.

"There is the responsibility of being an exemplar, to live what they are teaching. Next to be a cheerleader encouraging confidence that this is a meaningful path going beyond ego and toward awakening. Perhaps also to encourage anyone who thinks, 'I would like to try this out,' to sit down and look into their consciousness. We must share the teachings. It's like discovering a medicine that works and wanting to share that medicine with others."

John Pulleyn

"You know, Bodhin Roshi[67] and I have talked about this a fair amount," John Pulleyn tells me. "The teacher's job, really, is just to keep the student going. There's nothing the teacher can give the student, as you know. So, really it's just pointing out when they're going off the charts, encouraging them when they're discouraged, deflating them when they're too full of themselves.

"I really like the model – as I understand it – of the Chinese, where the teacher is like an older brother, and not like the Japanese where – as I understand it – the teacher is more like the *daimyo*, the Great Lord. You know, the teacher in that situation has a lot of power. That's one method. I think it probably depends on the nature of the student which one's gonna be better. For me, I always felt Bodhin Roshi was like an elder brother, even though I'm a year or two older than him. I didn't feel like there was a massive authority looming over me.

"And then, what can the teacher tell the student? I get students coming in who want to know, 'How do I do this? How do I do that?' And sometimes you can give them a little bit of help, but, in the end, they really need to work it out

---

67 Bodhin Kjolhede, Philip Kapleau's successor as abbot of the Rochester Zen Center. Cf. *Zen Conversations* pp.117-18; 146-47.

themselves. Even something as simple as, 'How do I look into a koan? How do I picture it?' Well, bang your head against the wall and see what happens.

"Roshi Kapleau said the mark of a good teacher is not helping the student too much. And when he died and was laying in a coffin in the zendo, and we went up to say our goodbyes, I said, 'Thank you for not helping me.' And I meant it."

Valerie Forstman

Valerie Forstman is the Guiding Teacher at Mountain Cloud in Santa Fe. She is also married to Scott Thornton. Valerie speaks extemporaneously with ease and can do so at length. Her response to my question about what Zen teachers teach is over nine minutes long without interruption.

"It is a lovely kind of conundrum question when asked in the context of Zen. My heart wants to respond to that, but I would like to preface it by pointing to a koan that I think many people reference when it comes to this teaching. Obaku[68] is railing at his monks, his students, 'You're all slurpers of dregs, drinkers of leas.' Then he says, 'I don't say there's no Zen; only that there are no Zen teachers.'

"I met with a student recently who's deep into this practice. At one point, she looked up at me and said, 'You're my roshi, but this ...'" – Valerie slaps the tabletop – "'... this is the teaching.' She got that. I'm fond of a saying attributed to the Buddha in the Pali canon, 'In this fathom-long body is all the teaching, all the Dharma: suffering, the cause of suffering, and the ending to suffering.' When I cite that passage, I often lift it up alongside a saying elsewhere in the sutras, 'The Dharma is beautiful in the beginning, beautiful in the middle, beautiful in the end.'

"In teaching, these twin statements are a placeholder for what this is, the Dharma functioning in some form of exchange. I do it all day long. Meeting students. Giving talks. Writing meditation tips. Leading a class. It's often an experience like holding up a mirror. Shining back. When teaching goes on, there's a clear reflection. When something happens, when there's a moment of recognition, when something gets exchanged or shared, it's the Dharma. The Dharma that wants to be shared. There's an energy in it, an outpouring. It's incredibly generous and energizing by nature. And it's always going on.

"I'm so grateful that we have the rich inheritance of teachings to draw on, to unpack, to look at from different perspectives. This great tradition. Often my own teaching is quite focused on what it is to be a human being. What it is to be alive. What is the present moment? What is *this*? And that points to

---

68   Japanese form of Huangbo.

suffering. Our world is broken, the wheel off its axis. I rarely give a talk without in some way naming that. And I feel that it is an invitation. I often say, 'Letting our hearts – our broken hearts – break all the way. All the way open.' One boundlessness. There's no other way I know.

"That, then, is what the tradition calls Wisdom and Compassion. This vast dynamism that is, at the same time, completely empty and utterly One. The one body – what Dogen calls, 'the true human body' – that we come to know in this fathom-long body. What a wonder!

"It's a joy and a gift to share this practice. That's what we're really doing. My own abbot – Yamada Ryoun Roshi – when he appointed me an Associate Zen Master, said, 'You're just a sherpa.' A companion. A guide. That makes sense and has been so helpful. I can see it in students, the value of having someone to sit with face-to-face, someone who's been on this path and can point the way; a kind of guidance that is particularly vital for koan training. Whenever that moment of recognition comes up, it's a taste of transmission; not something we 'get' but coming home to who we truly are. It's already here. It's *this*! There is recognition, but also a sense that we are sharing this world, that we're seeing this world together. That's an unspeakable joy."

Scott Thornton

Scott's answer is briefer. "Valerie and I often mention when we come away from a round of sitting with one of our teachers, and we go, 'Just sitting with that person deepens my sitting!' You know, there's some kind of power that they bring to the simple practice. It's either instructive or encouraging – to use common words – but it gets under my skin. I don't know how else to put that. They say things that are important too. When they give teisho, for example, these teachers are often taking a koan and – without giving the 'answer' to the koan – giving you this sort of window into it that, in the end, just points you back to yourself and your own effort to awaken.

"So, the teacher can encourage when needed, and tone down if somebody seems to be getting on a high horse. If I'm ever a full teacher, what I really hope I can help people do is keep it real. Keep it natural. It's just ordinary life here. We're not anything special."

James Córdova

Zen appeals to a fairly narrow segment of the general population. Zen practitioners, for example, tend to be college educated. A surprising number of Zen teachers are academics or psychologists. James Córdova of the Benevolent Zen

Sangha in Providence, Rhode Island, is both. He is the chair of the Psychology Department at Clark University and a licensed clinical psychologist. He encountered Zen while a student at the University of Washington.

"There was a professor, an addictions researcher. The University of Washington was full of bigshots, so mostly they didn't teach; they did their research. But if they ever fell into one of those gaps where they were between grants, then the university made them teach. This is what happened to him. He was in a gap between grants and so he agreed to teach a graduate course on the Psychology of Mindfulness which entailed meeting at his house at 7:00 in the morning and drinking overly strong coffee and browsing through his collection of Buddhist books and then sitting on his couches. He would try to teach us how to meditate, and then we would leave borrowing some of his books and hyper-caffeinated."

"And that got you interested?"

"It did. It really clicked for me. There were aspects of other things that had been compelling to me up to that point, including," he says chuckling, "existential psychotherapy and radical behaviorism. And there was a long interest in and exploration of – what? – a sort of spiritual quest, I suppose, that I fell into as I fell out of Catholicism and started to engage the journey of filling that space and meaning-making in that particular way. So of all the things I'd encountered, the stuff I was making contact with at that point about Buddhism and about Zen just consolidated it."

"And what does a Zen teacher teach?"

"That's such a good question. I think what a Zen teacher's function is is to create the conditions under which – with some guidance, right? – the conditions that nurture a growing clarity about intimacy. That we teach intimacy."

"That's an interesting answer. Does Zen have to be Buddhist?"

"I don't think so. That's not what's at the foundation of what is liberating about the practice."

"Do you present much Buddhist theory, talk about *kleshas*,[69] *skhandas*,[70] things like that?"

"Not so much, no."

Joshin Byrnes

"Well," Joshin Byrnes tells me. "I'm not sure I'm Buddhist. Maybe I am. I think of myself as a Zen guy." Joshin is an ordained Soto priest, so this is roughly

---

69 Conditions which defile the mind and hamper progress. These include the Three Poisons. See fnt 24, p. 30 above..

70 The elements that make up an individual's mental and physical existence: form, sensation, perception, mental constructs, and consciousness.

equivalent to a Jesuit saying he's not sure he's Catholic. Joshin is the founder and Guiding Teacher of the Bread Loaf Mountain Zen Community in Vermont. He is also active in Bernie Glassman's[71] "Zen Peacemakers" and continues the tradition of Street Retreats that Bernie had conducted, taking Zen students to live among the homeless as part of their practice.

"I mean, I don't know what qualifies one as a Buddhist. What appealed to me about Zen was that it was non-doctrinal, non-credal, non-dogmatic. I appreciate that about this practice. Zen is a radically inclusive practice. And I'm very heavily influenced by Buddhist teachings, but I'm in no way an expert. And I'm certainly not a cultural Buddhist from East Asia. You know, I like Buddhism; I like Buddhism a lot."

"The art's nice," I say.

"The aesthetics are nice; the art's nice. The teachings are compelling. It's kinda interesting. You know, I think of myself as a kind of an Inter-Spiritual New Monastic person."

"Which means?"

"Which means that I am committed to a rigorous spiritual life in the world and remain open to how wisdom arises in people. I am as moved by the teachings of Jesus and some of Jesus's followers as I am by the Buddha and some of the Buddha's followers. So for me, to quote Bernie, 'It's just my opinion, man.' I just don't feel comfortable locking myself into a doctrinal tribe. I'm a practitioner – you know? – and Zen is a practice, and it takes on many forms."

"Are you a teacher?"

"I am. Yeah."

"A Zen teacher?"

"Yep."

"So what does a Zen teacher teach?"

"Um ... How to appreciate your life."

"And how do you do that?"

"One by one."

Karin Kempe

I remind Karin Kempe, "You said that the underlying insight of Zen is not unique to Buddhism. In that case, I'm wondering, how important is Buddhism to the practice? If one can achieve the same underlying insight say, through Christian mysticism, how important is the Buddhist envelope?"

"I think when people have these insights, which can occur spontaneously,

---

71 Cf. *Zen Conversations*, pp. 28-29; 105-06; 137-40.

if they are not supported by a framework for their practice and development, they often fade away. Not always, but often that is the case. That's why it's useful to have a path to follow, a particular path. But I don't think my path's the best or only path. It's the best path for some people – best path for me – but not necessarily for everybody. There's an arrogance to think that we have the only door. I don't see it that way. And yet to practice within a sangha, to practice within a tradition that includes ethical teachings and ethical commitment and a progressive and supportive way to train, if you will – although we're not really training to be something else other than what we are – that seems to be very helpful for people."

Peggy Sheehan

Karin's co-director at the Zen Center of Denver is Peggy Sheehan. Peggy encountered Buddhism just prior to entering medical school in 1981. She was visiting a friend who was studying with the Zen teacher Lola Lee in San Diego. Lee had moved to San Diego to work with the early Zen pioneer, Henry Platov. During her visit, Peggy attended the practice sessions facilitated by Lee. And although she can't remember the exact words that Lee used in her first talk, the impact of what she said struck Peggy deeply.

"I think the difference, for me, that was so clear and heart-opening in that moment was that Lee was pointing to our 'original goodness' as opposed to the teachings of 'original sin' that I had grown up with in Catholicism. That resonated deeply for me, 'Oh, yes, you possess this original goodness that just needs to be touched and uncovered and experienced' in contrast to being brought up with a strong emphasis that we are originally bad and in need of healing."

"How important is the Buddhist envelope to Zen practice?" I ask.

"That's a really excellent question. I think it's not essential. I think many people are drawn to Zen and prefer not to consider themselves Buddhists. I guess I can go either way. My teacher, Danan Henry, used to say something at introductory seminars that I always appreciated. He'd say 'Well, you know, this is Zen *Buddhism*. This is a religion. And people in the west are trying to get away from religion. And yet, one of the translations for *religion* in the dictionary is "concern with the unseen." And we are very much concerned with the unseen.' And I appreciated that. I appreciated that there is a religious, devotional, mysterious part of this. Some people come to Zen as an intellectual pursuit. Or let's just say it feels comfortable in their intellect. Until, of course, it challenges things.

"People will ask me in the dokusan room, 'Where's the heart here?' When they're new and trying to get their practice established, and I relate to them asking that, because it's not always apparent. But I encourage them that if they stick with it, they will find it; they will find the heart here. But I also tell them that Zen is a wisdom tradition which is different from a *bhakti*[72] tradition. There are different entry points – there's the path of service, the path of devotion – all of these practices are entry points. So some are just more comfortable with entering in this way. And, of course, we all find and discover the commonality once we get into it."

"The commonality with what?"

"What the teachings are evoking in us. You know, it's the many paths up the mountain, but the view from the top is the same view."

"And where are these many paths going? What's the view?"

"Whatever tradition you enter, if you enter it fully, of course they are all going right here. They're all opening to a greater experience of this human life, and the truths and realities become – as we say – more vividly apparent. So whether it's opening your heart, opening your mind, I think it is the path to insight."

"So – what you didn't do, you didn't use the terms 'awakening' or 'enlightenment.'"

"Yeah," she says smiling. "I didn't say that because I don't like the words very much."

"So what does a Zen teacher teach?"

She reflects on the question a while before responding. "Of course, nothing. But ... I have an assistant teacher that I'm ready to think about transmitting to, and I realize it's such a silly thing to think about that. The only time you can think about that is when you're absolutely clear that there is nothing to transmit. It's just absolutely clear and obvious. And yet we have all had these wonderful teachers who have helped us along our way and with our journey."

"Is the term 'teacher' the problem? It's the word we use, but in fact I don't think I ever actually considered Albert Low my 'teacher.' That's not the right word."

"Yeah. 'Teacher' implies – number one – that there's a teacher *and* a student. I mean, I'm being taught every day by the people that I get to work with, the people who show up. So I think, yes, the languaging is a little bit off. And yet we do want an authentic teacher, meaning someone who has walked the path just a little bit ahead of you and helps show you the way."

"You said there is an assistant teacher you're considering transmitting to. Another term we use is 'mind-to-mind' transmission, which implies that the one receiving transmission shares – in some way – the same insight you have

---

72 Devotion.

and the same insight or the same way your teacher saw the Dharma. That there has been this continuous unbroken line of the people who have passed on this – for lack of a better term – insight. So, do you believe the insight you have as a 21st century woman – with a medical degree – is the same as that of an Indian sage who lived five hundred years before Christ and was so much a product of his culture and time that he doubted women should even be allowed in the sangha?"

She laughs. "I would love to say yes to that. But I'm still walkin' this path, and I think that fellow is a little farther ahead. But absolutely, if we have seen or touched this ground of reality or being – I don't like those words either – but this awakening, this enlightenment experience which then has to be lived and embodied and expressed, then, of course, it's going to be lived and embodied and expressed absolutely uniquely and differently in every human being. And, yes, that is what 'transmission' means. You have seen what I have seen; we have both touched this, and I'm satisfied that I can send you on your way. What's interesting is I've been a little bit reluctant to do a ceremony because I'm like, 'I got nothin'. What am I doing? What is this really?'"

"Well, is there not – since you accepted the role of being a teacher – a responsibility to ensure the continuance of the tradition?"

"Yes. Thank you for saying that. Yes. I sometimes shy away from some of these responsibilities which is a tendency that I have to work with."

"So, what are you looking for in an heir?"

"First a clarity in their own vision, the functioning of wisdom and insight, good humor, compassion and kindness, and the ability to help others, to encourage, to be an example. Ethical living is pretty important to me. And if somebody has been an assistant teacher that I've been working with as they work with students, you can feel it and sense it. It's like any kind of apprenticeship. I mean, even as a doctor, how do you hand this off? There's a lot of knowledge; there's a lot of stuff, but that doesn't make a doctor. So I think you're looking for a connection to this tradition, and the capacity to be able to come forth. And as I said, to be a responsible guide for others and to be an expression of the Dharma, the teachings that we all love so dearly."

Jeff Shore

"Does the Buddhist context for all this matter?" I ask Jeff Shore. "The Japanese cultural/religious envelope, does it matter? Could the practice be pursued outside of that context?"

"You certainly don't need to be Japanese or Chinese or Korean or Vietnamese, but it's very helpful to learn how it developed in China, naturally, because it's Chinese. How it developed in Japan. But we don't need to imitate those things."

"What about the Buddhism?"

"I would say you need to open up to Buddhism. I don't mean a card-carrying member, but I would say unless you understand in your bones the Great Matter of Life and Death, unless you see the suffering that you yourself cause as a human self, you cannot really do Zen practice."

"Koun Yamada, of course, fearing that Zen was fading in Japan, thought it might find a home in Catholicism. Do you think something like that's possible?"

He looks skeptical. "Mmm ... I would say you have to have some appreciation of the basic Buddhist principles. You don't have to believe in reincarnation. But you do need to understand what the Great Matter of Life and Death is. That it's not something apart from you. Perhaps the real question is whether such a mixing really plumbs the depths of either religious tradition.

"Maybe the best way to put it is the Buddhist matrix helps ground the practice. That's not something I had when I was young. Back then, I was desperately seeking some kind of an enlightenment, satori, kensho experience, 'cause then that would solve all my problems, but that attitude completely misses the basic teaching of Buddhism. At the same time that Buddhism teaches that there's a freedom from all conditions, it also teaches that within the self, conditioning is inevitable. You cannot get away from it. So you need grounding, some kind of awareness of the fact that I'm living in this world, I have certain responsibility. I cannot just, for example, not worry about anything that I do because when I become enlightened it won't matter anyway. This is a perversion of Buddhism. And Zen Buddhists often – myself included – have been guilty of that kind of thing. We've cut Zen off from its Buddhist base. Perhaps that illumines some of the problems in Western Zen today."

Kokyo Henkel

"Your time in Santa Cruz is coming to an end," I mention to Kokyo Henkel. "Somebody else will come and take your place. What's the job description?"

"Well, there is a job description of a couple of pages with a lot of detailed tasks. But it's a great question. I feel that meeting people in the present and responding to peoples' requests, whatever they might be, is the bottom line for a Zen teacher basically. But more than that, I have felt a responsibility myself to try to present the Buddhadharma in a rather traditional way. Dharma study is something that I've been personally really drawn to over the years. Understanding might be conceptual to start with, but it really does change one's experience and hones what one is doing in meditation. So I've felt a responsibility over these ten years at Santa Cruz Zen Center to try to present the full range of teachings both from the sutras and from Zen records. Especially Dogen's teachings, which are so rich and the basis of this lineage. And they're hard to understand. So that's been a big focus of mine, to try to lay that out in a kind of comprehensive and structured way. That's something I feel is important, and I think sometimes it's downplayed in Zen, conveying the understanding of the lineage through teaching the texts and discussing them together."

I ask what he sees the purpose of that study to be.

"If we're looking at Zen as something beyond just mere calm and peacefulness in the middle of a stressful life, it's really about changing our view of reality and deeply questioning all our perceptions and even dualistic perception itself. Mahayana Buddhist teachings are skillful and challenging in demonstrating how our ordinary daily life perception is actually completely deluded and inaccurate. And so these teachings, even if we don't fully get them, start opening us to the possibility that there's another way of being and perceiving and relating in the world that's quite different from dualistic perception and thinking. And the teachings come through words. You know, in Zen we have the koans and Dogen's unique language. I think it's interesting that Zen as a 'separate transmission outside the scriptures' has more written teaching than any other school of Chinese Buddhism."

4
ZEN AND PSYCHOLOGY

Scott Thornton

Scott Thornton, David Weinstein, Paul Cooper, and James Córdova are all psychotherapists or clinical psychologists as well as Zen teachers. "I can remember being in a day-long sit," Scott tells me, "and we always introduce ourselves, have a little round-circle at the end, and it's like, 'Is there anybody here that's not a therapist?'"

In the days before Zen became a practice in North America and was still largely a literary phenomenon – primarily based on the work of D.T. Suzuki – several eminent psychologists expressed admiration for Zen theory. Karen Horney became a personal friend of Suzuki. Erich Fromm organized an international conference with Suzuki on Zen and Psychoanalysis in 1957. And the pioneer Swiss psychoanalyst, Carl Jung, wrote the foreword to Suzuki's *An Introduction to Zen Buddhism*, although in it he argued that "a direct transmission of Zen to Western conditions is neither commendable nor even possible."[73]

Jung's reservations aside, not only has Zen been transmitted to the West, at times it appears that what draws people to Zen practice is similar to what draws them to therapy. How far those similarities go is a matter of opinion.

"I think people – and I know this was true for me – when they start meditating have a sense of something missing," Scott tells me. "It feels like I'm not living a life that's as joyful, as principled, or as helpful as I'd like to. And what gets in the way of our generosity and our compassion is this feeling of, 'I don't have enough. There's not enough for me.' There's a zero-sum game here. If you have something, I don't have it. If you have it, I'll get it. If I have it, you're out of luck. And I think there's a yearning, a fundamental yearning in people to drop that. They don't necessarily put it in those terms, but I think that it's there unconsciously. That's one reason people start practicing Zen. And people also come because they're hurting. They're struggling with anxiety, or they're struggling with depression, and they somehow feel that this will help."

---

73   Grove Press, 1964, p. 26.

"And what brings people to psychotherapy?"

"Yeah, that's real clear. 'I'm in deep pain. I'm depressed, suicidal, addicted. Scared. I'm angry.' Just fundamental human emotions that go awry. And, 'I know everybody gets angry; I know everybody gets anxious; I know everybody gets sad. But I can't get out of it, and it's getting worse.'"

"So either they or someone else has identified a condition, and they're seeking what?"

"A cure or palliative relief at least."

"How does that differ from what people coming to Zen are seeking?"

"Sometimes they come for similar reasons. And my teachers have been clear. It's not one or the other. If you struggle with relationships or whatever, if you're troubled by your past, you might need therapy, but keep sitting. Keep coming to meditate. But you might need a therapist too."

Later in our conversation, we discuss the skillsets required for therapists and for Zen teachers. For Scott they are distinctly different roles requiring different approaches and having different behavior protocols.

"As a therapist, I have to have a kind of professional detachment. There are certainly ethical aspects, guidelines, restraints in teaching as well, but it's a lot less. I can go to lunch with a Zen student. I can play music with them. I can help them take stuff to the recycle center. But I can't do that with clients. So there's an artificial separation. No dual-relationships in therapy."

What the two roles both require is empathy, a quality that can be acquired – it is one of the qualities Zen training is intended to arouse – but for some people it's inherent.

"Even when I was a teenager, my friends would come to me for advice. I seemed somehow to be calm, and they sensed a willingness to help and listen."

David Weinstein

"I spent lots of my spare time in high school sitting in my car listening to friends tell me their problems," David reflects, "wondering why they wanted to tell me their problems."

David sees a close relationship between his work as a psychotherapist and his role as a teacher of Zen.

"At this point, the only people I have in my psychotherapy practice are those who have a meditation practice already, are willing to start a meditation practice, or willing to discover that they already have a meditation practice, be it knitting or rock climbing. I am helping folks use their awareness as cultivated in their meditation practice to get in touch with the unskillful mind habits they have that are causing them difficulty. Perhaps most importantly, I help them notice how their negative judgements of themselves, based on what they are noticing, get in the way of change. Depending on the person, a koan can pay a visit also."

"So, both Zen and psychotherapy are ways of dealing with unhealthy mental habits?"

"Yes."

"What brings people to Zen practice?"

"Suffering."

"Always?"

"Yes, sometimes it's in the form of their relationships. There are many different versions of suffering, but the cause is always the same."

"What brings people to psychotherapy?"

"Suffering." I'd seen that one coming, and we both laugh gently. "Sometimes their spouse will literally bring them in as a condition for the relationship continuing. Sometimes initially people come in as an adjunct to the work their partner is doing individually."

"So, what's the difference? Why do some people choose psychotherapy and some people show up at the Zen Center?

"Well, psychotherapy can be just dealing with the issues that are coming up in someone's life that they want help dealing with, and they're not interested in existential questions. They're not interested in who they are, really; they're just interested in developing the tools and skills they think might be able to make their life more manageable and less difficult. Something like that. Some people come because they're troubled by something deeper. There's a woman I meet with who sought me out because she had not infrequent moments when she felt an intense connection with nature, and she was worried she was going crazy. I think she's surer now that, no, she's not going crazy. She's having a spiritual awakening. She's touching into the way we're all connected to everything. So, the people I have conversations with now who are seeking psychotherapy, whether they know it or not, are going to be working on that kind of a question. That's what my interest is. If it turns out that's not their interest, that's fine, it usually comes out in our introductory conversation and I suggest they look elsewhere."

"Is there a crossover? Do therapy clients become Zen students?"

"Not so much."

"What's the resistance?"

"I don't think of it as a resistance ... Well, maybe 'resistance' would be a word to use. It feels like a dispositional style. They don't tend to be joiners. The fact is Zen is full of folks who don't tend to be joiners. A lot of the people I talk with are creatively inclined, artists of one kind or another who appreciate that their art is their meditation, and it connects them in a way that meditation connects them also. They know that I teach meditation. Sometimes they'll ask, 'Can I come?' And I say, 'Yes. Sure.' I don't think anybody has come. Even when it's on Zoom and it would be so easy to come.

"Whether the conversation is about psychotherapy or about Zen – it is a conversation about what's coming up in their life, how their meditation practice is or is not helping, exploring how it is or is not helping, and not infrequently a koan will pay a visit and want to be shared. Sometimes it helps and sometimes it doesn't. There was a time when koan practice didn't help me too.

"I have conversations with a high school teacher in Oakland, an ex-NFL prospect who had a catastrophic hip injury and had to reassess his life and what he wanted to do with it. He knew what meditation is because that is what football was to him. He knew what practice is and how to condition and train himself. He came in one day very upset about an incident that happened at his school. As he was leaving school, he saw some of his students in a corner of the parking lot playing dice, which is not allowed on school property. He was disappointed, as they were some of his favorite students whom he thought knew better than that. He was also disappointed in himself for somehow having failed them. He broke the game up and lectured them. When he came in a couple of days later, he was still upset about it, ruminating about it. A koan came along to me as I listened to his story. It was about two friends down by a river. One friend sees two crows picking a frog apart. He turned to his friend and asks, 'Why does it always come to this?' His friend responded, 'It's only for your benefit.'[74] I told him that story because … I don't know, because it came to me, and I trust the way that happens. A week later he came in, and, as we were talking, he stopped and said, 'You know that story you told me last week?' I said, 'Yeah. The one about the crows.' He goes, 'Yeah, that one. Well, it's the damnedest thing. Ever since you told me that story, from time to time I find myself thinking about that scene in the parking lot and start picking at myself, and then that story comes along and I stop.' We talked about how that made sense to him in his life and the other things that he picks at himself about. That's the same kind of conversation I could have with a Zen student in a retreat. This guy is Christian. He goes to church; he has his tradition. But it helped him. Things like that happen."

"Do people who work with you as a Zen teacher have a different kind of relationship with you than someone doing psychotherapy has?"

"It depends on the people. I think since changing to working only with people who meditate, it feels like there is less and less of a difference. I notice

---

74   Case 98 of *The Record of Dongshan Liangji*.

that the people who I'm working with now who are meditating but came via *Psychology Today* or some other referral source are very grateful for their meditation practice and that gratitude overflows towards me for helping them with that. I didn't feel that so much as a straight psychotherapist working with people not using meditation that way."

I ask how he broaches the issue of meditation with his psychotherapy patients.

"The first thing I do is find out if they think that they already know how to meditate. I believe everybody knows how to meditate. I don't teach people how to meditate. We don't learn how to meditate, we *remember* how to meditate, because we're born knowing how to meditate. Zen mind, beginner's mind, literally. That we forget that beginner's mind is the issue. We forget that place that infants are in when" – he opens his eyes wide and smiles broadly – "they see that everything is everything! And then they're discovering, 'Oh! This is *my* thing.' We forget that. So, meditation is not something we have to learn, we just remember it, and we have moments of it all the time. When someone comes to me, I ask, 'What do you love?' For example, one person told me, 'I love rock climbing.' 'Tell me about rock climbing.' And they'll tell me about rock climbing. As they're telling me about rock climbing, I'm identifying in their story, 'That's meditation. What you're doing there. What you're describing to me, what's going on in your mind and your body and your heart when you're doing that.' Sometimes it's riding bicycles or motorcycles. It doesn't matter. Painting. Writing poetry. Whatever it is. I'm trying to find a place in their life where they already know what meditation is, and then when they can identify that, discuss ways they might be able to improve their ability to access that place. There might be techniques involved, but sometimes it's just a matter of noticing. The main technique is attention. You know, what Ikkyu said when asked what meditation is: 'Attention, Attention, Attention!'"

He is referring to an oft-quoted story about the 15th century Japanese master, Ikkyu Sojun, who was also a renowned calligraphist. On one occasion, a layman approached him, requesting him to write some words of guidance that could be hung on a wall. Ikkyu wrote the single word "Attention" on a sheet of calligraphy paper.

"'Attention?'" the layman read. "Could you elaborate?"

Ikkyu wrote a second time, "Attention."

"That's not much," the layman protested, uncertain whether his request were being taken seriously or not.

Ikkyu wrote one more time, "Attention."

"Okay, okay," the layman sputtered. "But what does 'attention' mean?"

"Attention," Ikkyu told him, "means Attention."

"How does that differ from what's going on in the commercial mindfulness movement?" I ask.

"I don't know. I have somewhat of a kneejerk reaction against the word 'mindfulness,' and then I notice myself doing that and the thought comes, 'You know, "mindfulness" gets a bad rap.' Many people are meditating and paying attention to their experience more now because of it, and that's great. People turn to mindfulness to get help, and they do get help with their chronic pain or their panic attacks and stuff. It helps; it really does. But there's a way of integrating this in your life that I don't hear mindfulness teachings talking about so much. When I say, 'Pay attention,' well, that's kind of like saying 'be mindful' isn't it? I encourage people to pay attention to their experience. 'What do you notice? What do you notice? What do you notice? What happened the moment before you noticed that?' I'm trying to cultivate the ability to notice the experience in finer and finer detail which helps in appreciating the texture of the experience. Partly for no purpose other than that there's something inherently enjoyable about paying attention. And – oh, yeah – it helps. Doing it because it helps is not a big enough, strong enough, deep enough kind of motivation to carry it on for a lifetime. Someone else came to Ikkyu looking for help, and Ikkyu's response was, 'Zen has nothing to offer.' And that 'nothing' is amazing. Hearing that, I'm encouraged. That Zen has nothing to offer other than what is, that is a miracle."

James Córdova

"The similarities between Zen and therapy are about the benevolent concern with suffering and addressing suffering," James Córdova tells me. "That's been a lot of what has drawn me to both. This sense of wanting to do something, to be of service. At least at the moment, I think the difference is … uh … Wow, what is the difference? … You know, psychology at the moment is really a little bit captured by – maybe a lot bit captured by – scientism. Right? So it has drifted away from acknowledging itself as a wisdom tradition and – if there's a cargo cult in here somewhere – is leaning more towards the forms of science. Which I'm big fan of. I fully subscribe to any methods that help us make sure that we're not fooling ourselves."

"Just to be clear," I ask, "are you saying that psychology has become more pharmacologically based?"

"Especially clinical psychology. We are still operating in a place where the shared view is about diagnoses, clinical conditions, treatments for clinical conditions, and the metaphor under that is you take a pill and determine how much of the symptoms did the pill relieve? And if we know what the mechanism of action is, that's great. If we don't know what the mechanism is, that's also great. So there is much less emphasis on experiences that have the potential to be more genuinely and whole-cloth transformative. It's about treatment of symptoms."

"What draws people to Zen today? When people knock on your door, what are they looking for?"

"A combination of things. One is suffering, their own suffering. And I think, too, what interacts with that is some hope – maybe? – some sense that there is a balm for their suffering that is in the more spiritual practice domain. Right? They're not seeking psychotherapy necessarily or singularly, and they're a little bit done with their own efforts."

"It's something they don't feel they can do on their own?"

"Yeah. They're seekers – right? – seekers of some sort of spiritual understanding and some way of holding the suffering that they're seeing and experiencing."

"And what draws someone to make an appointment with a psychologist?"

"They want to feel better. Just want to feel better. 'I feel like crap. I want to feel better.'"

"Is that significantly different than the other? 'I'm suffering; I want to stop suffering.'"

"I don't think they are significantly different, and I think that ultimately – at least in the way that I practice and the way some others practice – the overlap is pretty significant."

"They complement one another?"

"Yeah. They complement one another. But I think people enter the door with different metaphors in mind."

Seiso Paul Cooper

"About six or seven years ago," Paul Cooper tells me, "a colleague of mine – who's also a psychotherapist and a Buddhist practitioner in the Tibetan Dzogchen tradition – decided to organize a retreat that would be practice based. The structure of the retreat resembles a Soto Zen weekend sesshin. But the Dharma talk would be about some aspect of where psychoanalysis and Buddhist thought coincide. And the reason behind it is because there's been many conferences on Buddhism and psychotherapy, but there's typically no practice during those conferences. Generally, it's a group of the usual suspects, talking heads speaking to an audience. And what I've noticed over the years is more and more therapists have gotten interested in Buddhist practice and vice versa. There could be many people attending who might have something important or significant to contribute. So, we wanted to go into a dialogical type of format, but with an emphasis on practice. So we did that, and it was very successful. And we've been running one each year."

"By practice, you mean zazen?"

"Yeah."

"Presumably some of these psychotherapists haven't done sitting meditation before."

"That's right. I give an introductory talk on the practice of shikan taza – or just sitting – the preferred Soto Zen approach. And we have a few people available to provide private assistance to people if they're having trouble."

"And these sitting rounds are interspersed with discussions?"

"No. They're interspersed with brief periods of walking meditation. But we have a talk each day, and on one of the days we'll have an extended question and answer dialogue for maybe an hour or so. The rest of the time we're sitting. And recently more and more of the attendees have a Buddhist practice, have a contemplative practice of some sort and have been thinking about how they integrate the teachings – the Dharma – into their day-to-day therapy practice. So the dialogue feels like it's quite rich nowadays."

"What about psychotherapists who've never sat before, who are sitting for the first time, what do they get out of it?"

"I'm not sure I could answer that because everyone's different. Some people are looking for something and what comes to the surface is a discussion about explaining to people that zazen is not specifically or particularly a calming meditation. It's not a meditation that's going to put you into mystical states, and some people need to hear that. And some people don't listen to the instructions. Especially the body instructions. I tell people, 'We're not Spartans. If you're not comfortable, you're going to be focused on the discomfort, and that's not choiceless awareness. It's concentration. Concentration may be inadvertently on your knee or something, but, still, that's not the practice. So sit in a chair or stretch out your legs and do something.' But some people refuse to do that. I had this one person that was so uncomfortable that you could see the pain on her face. And by the end of the first day of the retreat, she just got up and left. And some people get to the end of the retreat, and they'll say, 'I had no idea! Wow!' And burst into tears. It's quite a varied response."

"What tools can therapists acquire from the Dharma?"

"At a practical and mechanical level, it helps people be able to sit with their patients more objectively, with more neutrality, with more patience, with more openness, maybe more presence. At a more subtle level, there's this concept in psychoanalysis that's called 'counter transference.' That has to do with the therapist's inner response or inner reaction to the patient, which in some psychoanalytical theories is seen as an obstacle, and others – theories I subscribe to – see it as more an intuitive awareness of the inner world of the patient."

"An intuition the therapist has into the condition of the patient?"

"It's an unconscious communication or process of projection – I'm trying not to get too technical with the language – where the patient's experience, often an experience the patient can't tolerate so they have to somehow evacuate it or get rid of it or communicate it unconsciously and the therapist experiences and feels it. And if the therapist isn't attuned to this it becomes subjective, and they could enact it in some way or another. But if we can take the subjective experience as an object, as information, we can learn something more about the patient's unconscious. And then, perhaps, be able to formulate that into words that will have a positive impact on the patient. I often call it a notation or an observation."

"What's the function of psychoanalysis?"

"For me it's a process of becoming more aware of who we are and how our behaviors might be influenced by internal forces, what we would call in Buddhism *samskaras*[75] or karmic formations or habit formations that we repeat over and over again. The simplest way I think about it is to create more elbowroom for the patient."

"And the function of Zen practice?"

"I think it does very much the same thing. I can be glib and quote Kodo Sawaki,[76] 'Zazen is good for nothing.' We might ask, 'What is this "nothing" that zazen is good for?' Dogen calls it doing a somersault. By which he means being more freely spontaneous and more flexible in our life and how that impacts our behavior in the world."

"Do similar things draw people to Zen and psychotherapy?"

"To me it's identical, and I base this on my own personal experiences. As a young person, I was suffering, and I didn't like suffering, and I wanted to heal it, figure out some way of getting past it. My life was very limited. I knew I had a lot of potential. The suffering was a source of severe depression. And I thought psychotherapy would help, and then I thought that Buddhist practice would help, and so I began to engage in both. To me it was a matter of survival. I think many people say, 'Oh, it's interesting' or 'I'm curious about it.' Collecting experiences. Whatever. But underneath it's because there's some feeling of dis-ease or suffering."

---

75   Mental impression, memories, and psychological tendencies which shape one's thought patterns.

76   20th Century Japanese Soto priest.

"Well, some sort of need at least. If one were totally content with the way things were ..."

"Absolutely. You wouldn't bother. Right? They're both tough paths. You'd have to be crazy to go through either of them unless you had some need or intent. To me Buddhist study and practice and psychotherapy practice is a like a Venn diagram. There are areas of identity, areas of similarity, and areas of deep difference. And I think some of the folks that I've encountered that come to Zen practice are really avoiding admitting they need psychotherapy and could benefit from it. The folks that come to psychotherapy practice, that's a wider range. I've noticed – and this only applies to people who've come to sanghas that I run – that they didn't fit in with the religion of their birth. Or they may be asocial or anti-social characters of one kind or another, but there's a need in them to connect with other like-minded people."

"What is it you hope for with your patients as a therapist?"

"That they could feel some ease or feel a little bit more emotional elbow room as I mentioned. That they're willing to take steps forward in their lives and maybe take some risks. You know, it's like one of the things I sometimes find myself saying, 'When you were a kid, you needed a lot of protection and maybe you don't need that same amount of protection now.' It's like when it's raining out, you wear a raincoat. But you don't notice that the sun is out, and you're still wearing your raincoat. Of course, you might need to carry an umbrella. You're going to need some protection, but not the protection you think you need. So, can you consider that? Can you imagine what that would be like for you? I'm not telling you to do it, I'm just telling you to imagine what it would be like."

"And as a Zen teacher, what is it that you hope for your students?"

"The same thing."

"You're just using different upayas?"

"Nowadays I've been calling it a little mindfulness and common sense. I don't mean mindfulness in the way that it's come to be popular. I should probably use a different word like 'awareness' or something. But be attentive to what you're doing and use a little common sense. Like during the pandemic, you don't have to avoid the supermarket if you wear a facemask and stay six feet away from the other people in the store as much as possible. But if you see another person down the aisle, and you're afraid to go down the aisle, I think you should question that a little bit. Like, what would be the common-sense thing to do. I think that could go a long way to easing everyday suffering. Just little things like that."

"Do the people who come to you as a therapist and the people who come to you as a Zen teacher have similar expectations of you?"

"No. And that's an evolution. So let me go back a few steps. Earlier in my career as a psychoanalyst if somebody wanted to learn how to meditate or something, I might suggest that they go either here or there. Depending on their personality, I might give them the name of a couple of centers that they could check out. Over time, especially after I had some publications, I had to start asking people, 'Did you want to engage me as a therapist or as a Zen teacher.' Depending on their answer, I would proceed in different directions. More recently what's evolved is people ask me if I could teach them how to meditate. They came to me for psychotherapy, but now they're asking about meditation. So it's a very different position now. I was much more boundaried – perhaps rigid – years ago about that. A classical psychoanalyst would be very critical of me doing this type of thing, but over the years my friends and colleagues have been saying, 'Why aren't you doing that? You're a teacher. You're depriving people.' I hadn't thought about it that way. I thought I was maintaining boundaries. But I won't proselytize or bring it up with a therapy patient unless they bring it up."

"So a therapy patient might also make use of you as a Zen teacher."

"Yes."

"And might a Zen student also make use of you as a psychotherapist?"

"Yeah, but that would be much more limited because I would also gear the talk towards understanding the Dharma and towards practice. So I'm not going to make a generic interpretation, which means simply bring up something from the past that gets played out in the present. I'm usually not going to do that."

"The impression I'm getting is that you have more freedom as a therapist to include Buddhist elements in your work than you have as a Zen teacher to include psychoanalytic elements."

"That's a good point. I hadn't thought about that. But that's true."

Erin Joen Dempsey

Joen Dempsey is a clinical psychologist in private practice. She is also a practitioner with Koun Franz's[77] Thousand Harbours Zen in Halifax. Koun himself has recently become a licensed therapist. For Joen, the goals of Zen and therapy are not the same.

"When I think about Zen, if a person has a goal when they sit down to do zazen, then there's something wrong with that picture already. That's how I've been trained and how I practice. 'Simply sitting' is the point of Zen. Being

---

77   Cf. *Zen Conversations*, pp. 44-45; 52-54; 87-88; 103-05; 134; 168-69.

present. Maybe it is like making friends with oneself. People talk about that concept in Zen, and it resonates with me; the idea of getting to know oneself – not in a discursive way wherein you're asking probing questions and responding internally – but wherein you sit and notice and see and are okay with what is inside. That's what I understand Zen to be about."

"So, without a goal. Does that mean purposeless? After all, why would you do it if it were purposeless?"

"Because it's honest. For me the reason to do it, despite there being no goal, is that it feels like an honest thing to do. It's a matter of being truthful with myself; I'm being authentic in the moment. I'm not avoiding; I'm not trying to escape. So, to be more in touch with the moment, to be more in touch with reality; these are important reasons to sit. With the caveat that if one sits down with the goal of getting in touch with reality then one is projecting oneself onto reality, which ultimately mediates one's experience and distances them from reality."

"What are the goals of psychology?"

"The goals of psychology are the goals of the person one is with. The goal is to understand a person's suffering and then help them to make changes."

"Are the things that draw people to therapy different from what draws people to Zen?"

"I'm told that there are people who are drawn to Zen because they have spiritual curiosity, or they're interested in enlightenment. Those goals tend to be different from those of the folks I work with. But someone might think, 'I have mental problems, so I want to go to Zen …'"

"Is that what people say when they go to a psychologist? 'I have mental problems, I need help.'"

"Sometimes. Usually, they come to you because they have a problem. And I started sitting in Zen because I had a problem. But in psychology, the problem has to be inside you. I can't help a person change the behaviour of their husband, for example. I can attempt to help a person with how they *respond* to their husband, and that might help their relationship. A person may come to psychology with an internal problem, but a lot of people don't. A lot of people come to psychology with an *external* problem, like the behavior of their husband. Then the job of the psychologist is to help the person see whether or not there is an internal problem that can be worked on to help them with their external problem.

"I've been thinking about this a lot because of the dual interest in my life. Zen opens a door to introspection, seeing oneself in context, seeing the patterns in one's mind, and seeing how one responds to others habitually. So Zen practice can be informative in a psychological way, particularly on retreat.

Or if interacting with people and anticipating responses from them that they have given no reason to anticipate, one can begin to see the ways in which past experiences inform perceptions of others. Basically, internal representations of others are based on how a person has experienced others in the past. Zen can help a person see those things, identify them, and understand them through meditation and through community. When people have a clinically significant diagnosis of depression, for example, Zen alone may not be sufficient to allow them to identify these patterns, because their internal representations of others may not be amenable to change without psychological intervention in some form."

Debra Seido Martin

Debra Seido Martin is a Zen teacher, a therapist, and an organic farmer. She and her husband, Bill Booth, operate Hortan Road Organics in Oregon, a working farm and apprenticeship program for people seeking to learn organic techniques. The farm is also the location of her Zen West Empty Field zendo.

"My life seems to have travelled in octaves. Eight years after graduating high school, I started my own farm, eight years later I entered Zen practice, and after another eight years I went to graduate school to become a therapist. It wasn't anything I'd aspired to. The motivation had been building though. At the Eugene Zendo, I was starting to lead small groups – 'Intro to Zen' kind of thing – and was confronted with things people shared that felt outside my understanding. People talked about severe depression, suicidal ideation in these groups, and abuse and I had no way of being able to respond to them. 'Just sit with it' sounded dismissive and inappropriate. I felt like something was really missing in the general psychological IQ of the setting. As for myself, even though I had cultivated a deep *samadhi* state,[78] there was something that remained untouched and unnamed. At the time though, it was common to disparage psychotherapy in Zen circles – still is in a way – as self-indulgent, ego-based, non-stop talk. You hear, 'Yeah, I've been in therapy for years. Doesn't work. Now I'm in Zen.'

"So I learned at the time, even though I'd been in therapy, to reject that line of inquiry. One day there was a panel presentation at the University of Oregon, called 'Psychology and Buddhism.' Very simple. I was like, 'I want to go to that! I'm interested! We don't talk about that.' One of the speakers was a woman who is now one of my formal Zen students. What was ironic was that I looked around the room, and about half of the people from our zendo were

---

78 A concentrated meditative state.

there in various little groups. They had all secreted off to this thing at the same time. I was fascinated by that.

"So I woke up the next morning with this clear voice in my head, which was completely preposterous given I was a fulltime farmer and on the eve of being transmitted. The voice said, 'You have to go back to school and get a degree in this.' I resisted it for a while. 'That's not practical. I mean, I have no time.' I felt called, but I also felt disloyal. When I told my teacher[79] about this, he quipped that he thought therapy was a 'neurotic solution to a neurotic problem.' I didn't blame him. He was my beloved and wise teacher. But there were points we didn't quite meet on. And on some level, I do agree with him. I'm not going to defend the profession. It's caused a lot of problems in our self-perception. *But* I still felt like I needed to go to do some healing in this realm.

"In hindsight, it's a no-brainer. I had deep pain inside that had remained hidden and untouched. At the time of this calling, I felt like I couldn't talk to any of my Zen teachers about this urge. So in order to get some guidance, I cold called the one guy I could find online who was a Zen teacher and psychotherapist, Joseph Bobrow in San Francisco. And he's written a book, *Coming to Life*. I said, 'I'm having this urge to go back to school, become a therapist, and I feel disloyal to my teacher and my tradition. Will you talk to me?'

"So I went down to San Francisco to meet him. I remember sitting in his office on Clement Street in the Richmond district and feeling nervous because I was so loyal to my Zen practice. He was very kind and said, 'You know, at first, you're gonna feel like you're going to go away from your practice. But in the long run, you'll be grateful.' That's all he needed to say. And I began to make moves to get into a graduate program. I had to go back and finish my abandoned undergraduate degree. I learned a lot about trauma and attachment. So many light bulbs went on. I soaked it up: group psychology, attachment theory, trauma, the nature of emotion, dreams. Now that I run a center, I cannot imagine being without this training and having to face people who are melting down, in crisis, conflict and grappling with unacknowledged trauma.

"*Dukkha*[80] is the common experience between Zen students and therapy clients. There are actually a number of therapies inspired by the teachings of Zen. Acceptance and Commitment Therapy and Dialectal Behaviour Therapy really lean into the Four Noble Truths. They help people stop seeking happiness in a place it's not found. Even though a therapy client may not be interested in spiritual practice, I often see the way-seeking mind in all beings, no matter how nascent. There's an impulse, to resolve something – resolve an

---

79 Kyogen Carlson in the Jiyu Kennett lineage.

80 Suffering. See fnt 10, p. 17 above.

existential question – in the worst of behaviors. I think of clients who face a life-threatening diagnosis. They're coming to therapy because they don't know what to do. The old identities fall away, and they are looking directly into the question of life and death. Actually some of my clients who are not Buddhists come in with the most beautiful dreams, original koans, and Buddhist insights right off the bat. That's true of people in addiction treatment too. They often directly understand they're not going to get a release from this substance and can map that insight onto other experiences in their lives."

I ask if there are people who come to her for both Zen and therapy.

"That's a common discussion in Zen teaching circles because so many of us are also therapists. Most agree it's good to separate these roles, to avoid the dual role of being someone's Zen teacher and psychotherapist, roles that can come into conflict with each other. You also then assume too much power in someone's life when they are vulnerable. I've made a couple of considered exceptions when someone ends therapy and wants to then take up Zen, or vice versa, but it comes with complications. So I do keep my therapy practice separate from the zendo, even though they're in the same building."

"Are there similarities in the way you work with the two groups?"

"As a therapist, I offer a different kind of medicine that's complementary to Zen training. Therapy helps heal the broken relational field and the inner disconnection and numbness that come from trauma. As a therapist, I walk into the someone's very particular 'karmic' conditioning and offer new ways to experience themselves as fundamentally loved and welcome in the world. There is a lot of reparenting, learning to trust, to be a fair witness to one's life, to love, and to face conflict. In Zen, this kind of integration is vital but not always tended. As a therapist, I'm tracking the progress of a client in a different way than I would a Zen student. I'm much more wide open about where the Zen student is going. There's a bigger field for the Zen student to roam."

"The Zen students have a bigger field?"

"Yeah."

5

THE IMPACT OF ZEN PRACTICE

Debra Seido Martin

"What do people get out of it," I ask Seido.

"What do they get out of it? If people follow the practice, they are met with what is needed. For one person, that may be a moment of profound release from an old karmic burden, for another, a kind of surrender into something larger than themselves, trusting a new instinct. The insights that come are endless. I'm always in awe of Zen's wisdom about this. Many people who come to Zen and stay say they feel at home in the silence. It reminds me of the Buddha's story, when he walks around the bodhi tree. In the south, west, and north, the world tips out of balance, but when he faces east, he finds solid ground to sit upon.[81] That's a profound discovery in someone's life. A zendo faces east. You're given a seat and the tools and the empowerment to answer a question that you're carrying. In many ways, that question is like an onion. Sometimes on the surface it's, 'I don't know what I'm doing in my life' or 'How do I face this relationship problem?' That's the surface. Zazen allows you to sit with that and peel back the layers. And that takes time and steady practice."

"How does it do that?"

"How does it do that? The silence does that."

"And the teacher's job is what?"

"To keep them going. This teaches trust. You have to rely on the 'don't know' mind. It's profound. 'Refuge' is our more formal word for it; something other than what you've been trusting until this moment. Something you don't know. But kind of know. You have to lean into practice, not keep it at arm's length. I like to use the hammock metaphor. Sure, we can sit in the hammock, but if you don't release your weight into it, trust it, it's really uncomfortable and you never find out what it's really for. But if you can soften into being held by that hammock, something begins to shift and move. And that's a mystery."

---

81 She is referring to the story of the monk Gautama taking his seat beneath the Bodhi (Wisdom) Tree, where he attained full and complete enlightenment – *unuttara samyak sambodhi* – and became the Buddha or Enlightened One.

Julie Nelson

Although she tells me she doesn't consider herself so much a Buddhist as a Zen practitioner, Julie Nelson is the Teaching Coordinator at the Greater Boston Zen Center.

Her introduction to meditation came at a time when – as she describes it – her life was "falling apart." Her marriage was dissolving, and she was engaged in a dispute over tenure at the university where she taught. She felt a general panic about things. "How was I going to support my kids! Where was I going to get a job! I couldn't just move anywhere in the country; my kids were in joint custody. I had to find a job in my field in this area. Find a place to live. Deal with all the emotional repercussions of that, deal with the lawsuit."

She was also scheduled to have surgery and took part in an adult education workshop intended to help people prepare for surgery and to heal more quickly afterward. The workshop included some guided meditation. "The interesting thing was that I found as I sat quietly listening to the guided meditations – or even without them – I could watch my panic rise up and fall away. And that was very powerful because I would have thought I *was* my panic, was living from my panic, was panic all the time; but sitting quietly I could see it as something that arose and left."

After the surgery, she decided to investigate meditation more thoroughly. "I got some books, and for the next few years I did some meditation at home just on a kind of as-needed basis. Ten minutes here; five minutes there." One of the books was by Larry Rosenberg of the Cambridge Insight Meditation Center in the Vipassana tradition. "I went to a few retreats there. I was a member there a couple of years. Didn't get there regularly. I found the teachers relatively inaccessible. That is, they would only teach group things. You had to be a very senior student to get a one-on-one meeting with them." When she applied for a personal interview, she was given an appointment six months off.

Then she learned about James Ford who was then teaching at the Henry David Thoreau Zen Sangha in Newton, affectionately referred to by its members as "Hank." Once a month, James offered dokusan to anyone who wished to attend, whether they were members of Hank or not. That was one appeal. Another thing that struck her during her first visit to the community was the chanting of the Five Reminders:

> I am of the nature to grow old. There is no way to escape growing old.
> I am of the nature to have ill health. There is no way to escape ill health.
> I am of the nature to die. There is no way to escape death.
> All that is dear to me and everyone I love are of the nature to change.

There is no way to escape being separated from them.
My actions are my only true belongings. I cannot escape the consequences of my actions.
My actions are the ground upon which I stand.

"That grabbed me. You know?" Julie says. "Here's a group of people that face facts. I found that very appealing.

"So what does Zen do? There's probably two levels, an entry level and a deeper level. The entry level is it does usually give you a chance to calm down your mind. Which brings a lot of people in the door. So there is that sort of counteractive to an over-active brain aspect and maybe over-active emotions. The deeper aspect is if you sit long enough you end up looking into the stuff you've been avoiding, and you can grapple with your life as it is in a more honest way. People who have been in therapy might relate it to that. Uncovering some dark things and some hidden beliefs can be helpful in untying knots that make you misbehave and make your life more difficult. And then Zen takes it somewhat further than that."

"In what way?"

"Mostly by helping us take ourselves less seriously," she says with a laugh. "When you get right down to it. This old ego, this old selfing, when you back up a little bit, give it less energy, life is not such a huge problem and burden anymore."

"What about awakening? Isn't that what Zen is supposed to be all about? Changing your whole way of seeing and relating to things?"

She frowns. "The experiences of no-separate-self shake you all the way down through the soles of your feet and beyond, but it's more a matter of scale than seeing something different. 'Cause really what you're seeing is what you're seeing all the time. That I am not some entity unto myself. I'm the breakfast I ate this morning. I'm the air that somebody sitting across from me just exhaled. I'm two or three pounds of bacteria, or so we're told. I'm what I was taught by my parents. This interdependence of things is factually all around us. We just have habits of not noticing it."

Meido Moore

"There is a Japanese word – *shugyo* – that is very important," Meido Moore tells me. "Of all the various words in Japanese that can be used for some kind of training or practice, shugyo is considered the most profound. We usually say that it implies the deepest possible psycho-physical or whole-being training: a unified physical and spiritual training engaging the whole body-mind. What people get from Zen training is the orientation of their lives to become shugyo. Average persons, common people, view life as an environment or a set of conditions and circumstances that are sometimes desirable, sometimes afflictive, and spend most of their energy trying to push away conditions that are afflictive, hold onto ones that are desirable, and so on. All the while, they blame these conditions or other people or the environment for their own angst, their own discomfort. But shugyo is a completely opposite kind of orientation. The mind of shugyo, or training, is one in which whatever I encounter – people, conditions, circumstances, whether so-called 'inner' or 'outer' – are used as a mirror. Anything that is uncomfortable to me, that is challenging to me, that scares me or gives me angst, I use then as a way to look at myself, to see my weaknesses clearly, and so then to refine, change and transform.

"Let me describe it this way. If the conditions of life are like a grindstone, most people do this." He drives the tips of the fingers of one hand into the palm of the other. "Like blunting a blade perpendicularly against the stone. Right? The approach of training or shugyo we get from Zen, because of the deep psycho-physical orientation of the training and the way it teaches us to work with conditions, is that whatever we encounter, we don't blame those conditions at all. We use them to sharpen ourselves." He slides the fingers of one hand along the palm of the other, as if honing a blade. "Refine. Refine. Refine.

"So I guess speaking in the most simple way – without talking about awakening, kensho, liberation, and so on – but just regarding the practicality of the practice path, it's an approach to life in which whatever we encounter is an opportunity for refinement, knowledge, and wisdom – for strengthening and self-development – rather than judging things as 'positive' or 'negative' and assigning blame. Whatever makes me uncomfortable, it becomes a question of 'Why am I uncomfortable?' Not, 'Why is this happening to me?' It's a very different orientation.

"Of course, it doesn't mean that we shouldn't speak up when circumstances and occurrences are unjust or incorrect. But it means that when I encounter anything, I have a choice how I will use it to refine myself. I think that sums up the kind of change in orientation that people get from Zen training. Even if they do not call themselves Buddhists, they might still be able to get that – that change in orientation – and use that in their lives. It makes such people uniquely, I think, useful to others, and inspiring to others."

Roger Brennan

Roger Brennan speaks slowly and with care when the issue of kensho comes up. "I don't ... I have not found people who have had kensho necessarily ..." – he pauses to consider how best to express himself – "... to be people that I would consider to have been transformed."

I agree that it is disappointing to see people who were acknowledged to have had an awakening experience and yet still had pretty messy lives.

"I wouldn't necessarily go that far," Roger says. "I wouldn't necessarily even know about their personal life. But I would say about their attitude towards life. They're not necessarily happy. They're not even necessarily particularly nice people."

That is true. And it's also a fact that sometimes they do have messy personal lives.

Even lineages which emphasize the importance of kensho recognize that in itself awakening does not necessarily bring about a change in character. And it is not just an issue of students who achieve kensho but then fail to integrate it in a meaningful way in their lives. In 2013 – the year I began undertaking the interviews upon which many of my books have been based – a book was released by *New York Times* writer Mark Oppenheimer entitled *The Zen Predator of the Upper East Side* in which he detailed the inappropriate sexual behavior of Japanese-born Zen teacher Eido Shimano in New York City. Later that same year, Oppenheimer published an article in the *Times* – just a few weeks before I began my tour – about 105 year-old Zen Master Joshu Sasaki who had been sexually interfering with female students during private interviews for decades. These two were not alone. By the beginning of the 21st century, there had been numerous revelations of a range of abuses of authority by Zen teachers. The reactions of individual sanghas ranged from indifference – which appears to have been the case in Providence – to demands for the teacher's resignation, which occurred in San Francisco.

The more fundamental issue, however, was how people acclaimed for their spiritual insight could misuse their positions as egregiously as these men had done.

Zenshin Michael Haederle

In February 2013, in a column on the front page of the *Albuquerque Journal*, Leslie Linthicum described the impact that the revelations of Sasaki's behavior had had on her family. Her husband, Zenshin Michael Haederle, had been active with the Albuquerque branch of Sasaki's school for more than twenty years. Like many people associated with Sasaki, he had heard rumors that the Japanese-born roshi occasionally tried to fondle female students during private interviews, but he assumed that it was something that had occurred in the past and was due, at least in part, to a matter of cultural differences.

In September of 2012, Zenshin had been asked to be the resident administrator of the Albuquerque Center. He and his wife prepared to rent their house and move into the living quarters at the Center. That November, an article on the now-defunct *Sweeping Zen* website revealed the full extent of Sasaki's behavior which was continuing and went beyond groping. As Leslie's article pointed out, no one associated with Sasaki's primary center, Rinzai-ji in Los Angeles, or with his retreat center in New Mexico disputed the allegations, and Sasaki himself remained unapologetic. By December Zenshin and his wife canceled their move. He disassociated himself from Sasaki and withdrew from the community to which he had been committed for so long. He now hosts a small group of practitioners who support one another without a resident teacher.

Zenshin is what is called a "lay monk" in Rinzai-ji language. "It's weird terminology. Some people have pointed out that none of the Zen clergy in Japan really qualify as monks, because they can be married, and they don't take most of the monastic precepts that are embedded in classical Buddhism. A better term in English might be 'priest' or 'minister.'"

I ask if he considers himself a minister.

"Maybe. In the sense that I'm leading a Zen sitting group and provide some guidance there, although I certainly don't consider myself a teacher. To me it's just a commitment to make the Dharma available for people."

The conversation inevitably turns to Sasaki and other teachers who were considered enlightened and – perhaps more to the point – were capable of guiding others to some degree of awakening, and yet could be guilty of inappropriate sexual or financial behavior, substance abuse, and personal aggrandizement.

"Awakening is a profound experience," Zenshin tells me, "although it's not exactly an 'experience,' right? It's a profound *something*, because 'experience' presupposes an 'experiencer.' It's not an intellectual insight. I would say awakening holds enormous transformative potential. I kind of liken it to a very bright spotlight; with awakening what's in the spotlight becomes very clear. But the way our personalities operate, including the ways in which many people are raised or conditioned, we have these very sophisticated ways of hiding things from ourselves. So in a sense, these things remain outside of the spotlight. And that's where tools like psychology or some kind of wise introspection, or maybe just a kind of unflinching relationship with someone else who will call you on your shit, can pull those things into the spotlight so you can see them. Once they're in the spotlight, then they can dissolve. Like anything else, their empty nature becomes apparent. But you have to be able to see them in the first place. And I look back now on Joshu Sasaki Roshi's example but also on plenty of other people who were raised in societies where psychological introspection as we know it in the West was literally not even a concept. All kinds of things could be operating in their personalities, but they weren't aware of it, essentially. There's kind of blinders. You could be very deeply awakened, but you still have the blinders on. It calls to mind the expression from Torei Enji[82] regarding the 'long maturation,' the idea of continually realizing that your delusions are truly numberless. You have to keep working. And you have to be open to that."

We discuss current social conditions, the climate crisis, a resurgence of racial unrest, political polarization, all of which results in many people feeling anxious. I ask if Zen practitioners are any better equipped to deal with these matters than others might be.

"One of the things that I really appreciate about Zen practice is it's all-encompassing. It's kind of a tool, if you want to think about it that way, that's applicable to anything we encounter in life: aging, sickness, death, all the traditional things. It also applies to what's going on in our society. It's obviously not about nihilism or zoning out or shrugging your shoulders and saying 'whatever,' but it is about meeting whatever's going on with clarity and equanimity so that your response is going to be appropriate to the circumstances.

"So it's not about leading with an opinion or mentally freaking out, but it is about having a fuller appreciation for the totality of the situation you're actually in, *this* moment and not all the other moments in your imagination. Obviously that's a challenge, but that's the aspiration. It's not that anybody can do that freely all the time, but it's a great place to start, because it's so easy for our emotions to take front and center, our emotional response to political bullying and injustice, the crazy disregard for objective truth and facts and things like that. I mean, it's all really disheartening for a lot of people. But then also just working with that, working with our own anger or despair or all the other related emotions. Those are real, in their way. It's a matter of meeting these circumstances in a way where we don't go out to the gun stores and get our own arsenal to match the arsenal on the other side or something like that. We want to get outside of that mindset, that paranoic conflict.

"This is where the benefit of long-term practice comes in. We become more alert to our mood states, to whatever is coming up in the moment. You realize you can do something about that. You can take a look at this whole personality complex that seems to be having this problem – this whole neurotic story-telling thing – and more or less see through that pretty quickly. Where years ago I might be hung-up for days, weeks or months on some kind of conflict or afflictive emotion – because I was pretty neurotic – now it's more often hours or it's minutes. Literally, the drama loses its attraction. I can more readily

---

82   17th century Japanese Zen Master.

see that going down the rabbit hole of ruminative or obsessional thinking is just a waste of time."

"You're not identifying with these feelings as they arise? Is that what you're saying?"

"That's a way of putting it. Because fundamentally there's no one there to identify. Identity becomes a highly suspect concept. Emotions come up; it's not like suppressing or repressing anything. It's just allowing it all to be there and allowing it to go away and not fighting with it.

"Fundamentally, emotion is just a pattern of sensations in the body and a characteristic complex of thoughts. Actually, to consciously move into the body – to that felt sensation regarding whatever is going on – is a great solvent. I always think of how easily our animal friends do this. A dog barks at the mail carrier and acts like it's going crazy. Then the mail carrier goes away, and the dog goes back to wagging his tail because he doesn't sit there and question the appropriateness of his response. The dog has no self-image that he's trying to manage. The dog is just in the moment. Emotions arise; emotions pass away. They're not anything to worry about. Again, it's a process. It's not like I never say or do something inappropriate, but it feels like there's a lot less of that than when I was younger.

"Maybe it's all a function of getting older. Psychologists say that people in general get happier as they get older and develop greater acceptance, but I think it's more than that."

Karin Kempe

"I can only speak for myself," Karin Kempe reflects. "I was a miserable 20-year-old. Maybe I'm a happier 72-year-old because I'm now 72. But I can't help but think that a lot of the joy that I experience in the simplest things of life is somehow related to practice despite the fact that I still don't particularly like sitting still. I'm restless, and I have physical pain. I still have a wayward mind. In spite of all that, I really, really appreciate this life. And the painfulness of the pain that I experienced in my own mind in those early years, that did lift and go away."

I ask what she means by the pain in her mind.

"During my early years, especially in Rochester, I think I just cried for several years in the zendo. I learned later that they called me the 'weeper.'" She can smile at the memory now. "I experienced a lot of internal pain, and my mind felt painful to me. Maybe it was self-doubt, which was paralyzing for years. But it really did resolve and open up for me. So, what do we get through practicing? I think we experience a bigger more inclusive way of seeing ourselves and others and our circumstances and our world. And it's not that we don't get cancer or a heart attack or that we don't lose our best friend. But the way that we enter into that reality has somehow softened, has become part of our being fully human and having the gift of walking on this Earth." She pauses, then adds, "It's an amazing thing."

James Córdova

James laughs gently when I ask what people get out of Zen practice.

"I hope they come away with more of a sense of humor." It's a surprising answer. The traditional portraits of Zen masters found in art from China and Japan are often of individuals so dour looking their glance – as the saying goes – could curdle milk.

"That picture of Bodhidharma," James chuckles. "Just scowling! Right?"

"So what do you mean by saying that you hope they come away with a better sense of humor?"

"I think there's a lightness, a presence, a playfulness that, for me, is one of the hallmarks of intimacy, one of the hallmarks of a thorough-going coming-to-terms-with, 'Oh! This is what it's like to be a human being.' And that sense of community and that sense of common humanity that comes with that, and the letting-go-of, the putting-down-of the struggle, it's a little bit like being let in on the joke."

Chris Amirault

Chris Amirault is a practice leader with Shining Window Zen in Tulsa. When I ask if being a "practice leader" puts him on tenure track, he says, "You know, that's part of what I'm trying to figure out, whether I am on tenure track, and how you square that with 'no attainment.'"

His view of practice is necessarily a little different from that of fully authorized teachers.

"There's lots of different ways that we inhabit this practice. I like what Shitou Xiqian[83] wrote hundreds of years ago, 'Turn around the light to shine within and then just return.' That's the practice. The practice is developing a sense, an ability, a mindset, a perspective that allows you the opportunity to develop an awareness of what you are aware of. So, turning that light around to shine within and then turning back to the world and returning back to your seat and returning back to other people and your job. So our practice is to be really mindful of the fact that if we turn the light around to shine within,

---

83   8th century Chinese Chan master.

there's lots of fascinating things that we can learn that we might not have seen before, and they can help us go about living our lives in a more engaged and compassionate and wise way."

"And what would living like that do for me?" I ask.

"I have no idea. Look, all the research on happiness is very clear on this point. Which is that people who do what I just described tend to be less happy."

"Tend to be *less* happy?"

"Yes. People who describe themselves as concerned with social justice or as self-reflective or ask themselves questions about the meaning of life, those people – on the whole – tend to declare themselves to be less happy than people who say, 'Fuck it. I don't care about any of that stuff. I'm goin' to go get my this and buy my that.' So this is why the Buddha sat under the tree, as far as I'm concerned. Right? So the question then becomes, 'Well, if getting happy isn't the outcome, what's the outcome?' And I think the outcome is a different way of engaging with and holding the world and yourself in it. And that includes feeling suffering. Zen Buddhism isn't an analgesic. It's not heroin. When I'm talking about the practice, when I say, 'More engaged,' I mean 'More engaged with *this*.' This practice is not going to transform everything into glorious dancing sprites. Suffering is suffering. The world really is burning. This, sadly, is not a metaphor. Fascism and hate are on the rise. And, by the way, you do have anxiety, and you do have pain and suffering, and you're going to get old, and you're going to get sick, and you're going to die. Right? And Buddha was right, those three things are hard to deal with. So what the practice offers is an opportunity to engage with what life presents us in a thoughtful and compassionate and wise way that allows us both the opportunity to be deeply in the experience as it unfolds and to recognize more broadly a capacious, more boundless sense of what reality is as well. And that ain't for everyone."

Cynthia Kear

Many of the people with whom Cynthia Kear works have had difficulties with addiction – as she admits she had as well – and are in recovery. For them, the desire to relieve suffering is a common entry point.

"And I don't think it's off base. The Four Noble Truths are exactly about that. There's suffering; there's causes of suffering; and there's transformation of suffering. What zazen allows you to do is to settle yourself on your self so you get to see clearly what's going on. My own very deep affliction was being a very fear-based person which my teacher helped me understand, and that came out of the causes and conditions of my family life. So sitting zazen I could get in touch with both reflecting on experiences, thinking about future conversations, feeling my heart clench or my belly clench. I could get in touch with my fear and start to settle myself, settle the self on the self and relax into that and become a little bit more aware of it. And with encouragement and support, I could see the arising and the falling of that; see that it is temporal, and it can be changed.

"The type of suffering I deal with, both personally – that I've dealt with in my life – and with my students, is deeply, deeply entrenched. I mean, we're talking about people – not all of them, but many of them – who come from very dysfunctional, disturbing, traumatic backgrounds. This is in them at a cellular level, and it takes a really long time. So learning to sit with their actual experience and see it and try to see it as zazen teaches us to see it with a kind of backwards step. A little neutrality. 'Oh! Look! There's Cynthia being scared again. Why? There's fear rising in the belly. Why?'

"I think it is the understanding that we all are Buddha Nature. I find that very helpful for myself and for other people that have had a lot of suffering and trauma and whatnot. 'Wait a second! You are Buddha Nature. You just have to remove the obstacles and start trusting and manifesting and expressing it in a skillful way.' Which is where the Precepts are helpful."

Jean-Luc Foisy

Jean-Luc Foisy informs me that after the death of Albert Low, the Montreal Zen Centre went through "an inevitable period of confusion, wondering, what are we going to do? A lot of people had relied on Albert's presence. He was the center of the Centre. He was the founder, as you know, and what he built is quite remarkable. The way he dedicated his life to the teaching, the books he wrote, the time and energy and effort he invested created what I guess we call in our language a 'Dharma.'"

Towards the end of Albert's life, Jean-Luc served as his attendant, "helping him physically to go to sit for the dokusan to meet the people, to go to the zendo when he was still doing the teishos. And I could appreciate the pain and the difficulty that he was going through. And also his stubbornness, his determination to carry on until his last breath. It was quite remarkable.

"The fact that he did not appoint a successor left most of the members in an unknown zone. And I find that was actually pretty wise of Albert." He smiles and chuckles softly. "It's a good way, especially for the long-term members to reflect on the question, 'Are you in or not? Are you willing to carry on with this in spite of the difficulty? Are we able to work this out together?' And if not, you might as well move onto something else, and that's what many people did, to be honest. I was determined to stay. I have a great deal of gratitude and utmost respect towards the work Albert and Jean, his wife, did. It would be a shame to just let it disappear."

One of the things I remember Albert frequently reminding his students was that Zen has nothing to offer the personality; therefore, to ask what one gets from the practice is problematic.

"You see, it's a very delicate question," Jean-Luc notes. "We have all heard the story of Emperor Wu who had done considerably to support Buddhism in China. When he asked Bodhidharma, 'What is the merit for all that I have done?' Bodhidharma replied, 'No merit sir!'

"We all come to practice with a shopping list, with expectations. It is important to have the humility to recognize that and work with it. To carry on in spite of all the difficulties and frustrations for as long as it takes, until eventually one gets a glimpse of what this is all about. From that day on, the very notion of merit disappears. This fixed point of view of self and others – me and the outside world – is momentarily shattered. We know from within the very meaning of a prostration, and we serve in accord with the spirit of the first vow. You engage with the mystery of life which remains unknowable but is no longer an abstraction. You're not going to get anything out of this, life will. It is this on-going process of life – this 'dynamic unity' as Albert called it – that you engage with. You yourself don't have any idea what direction it will take. You make mistakes, you continue to struggle with the habits and inclinations of your personalities. No, there isn't anything for you to get out of this, but it does, definitely, unfold. It is like a flower blooming. That is a good metaphor for describing the process of awakening, in my view anyway. The *actualization* of the awakened mind, I would say."

Gyokuko Carlson

Gyokuko Carlson is the retired abbot of the Dharma Rain Zen Center in Portland, Oregon, which she co-founded with her husband Kyogen, who died in 2014. The two met at Shasta Abbey, the primary teaching center of the Soto teacher, Jiyu Kennett. Although Gyokuko served as Kennett's attendant for a period of time, she tells me that it was less Kennett herself than the abbey and its schedule which became her teacher.

"I felt that I was being immersed and disciplined into a way of life that was structuring my mind. We sometimes say about the meditation posture that you're using the body to direct the mind. And I felt that everything in the schedule and the method of being, the deportment, it was all there to direct the mind."

"To what end?" I ask.

"Clarity in general. I think in my case coming to a realistic and holistic sense of self. A sense of this person being integrated into a larger whole. So I suppose being in community is actually a model for that. You were given a place, a rank, a seat at the table, a seat in the zendo, and you have the integrity of that place, but you also have a responsibility to the whole of the zendo, the whole of the lecture hall, the whole of the community. It's the model or the microcosm for a larger sense of being a piece, an integral piece, of the whole of the universe. I think one of the gifts of Zen practice is a sense of what Roshi Kennett used to call 'natural pride,' a sense of self-worth that is not larger than anybody else's and does not supersede anybody else's but is the basis of respect for all things, that puts you in relationship to all things. I had this sense once walking down the cloister and just being centered in my own breathing and having the sense that my in-breath and my out-breath was the same in-breath and out-breath as the whole of the Earth beneath my feet. And it was not powered by me, and it was not *not* powered by me."

Michael Leizerman

Michael Leizerman is a formal student at the Buddhist Temple of Toledo, what in their parlance is called a *shoken* student. Rinsen Weik explains the step as one in which the student and teacher have a covenant, "an agreement about our relationship and how it's going to work and what it's about, and it's a very clearly defined thing. Now we're going into the deep end of the pool together."

Michael is also a lawyer and co-wrote a book entitled *The Zen Lawyer*[84] with Rinsen. When he tells me that the law is his Zen practice I suspect at first it is one of those hyperboles Zen practitioners can fall prey to, but it turns out to be a simple statement of fact.

At one point in our conversation, we discuss the concept of "practice," what it means to say that one "practices law" or "practices Zen."

"Practice means 'to put into action.' To practice law is to put law into action. To practice Zen is to put Zen into action, to put reality into action. I've thought a lot about that word. Let me start with the 'practice of law.' There's a little bit of humility in it maybe – right? – that you can't get it perfect, that you're always practicing. On the other hand, I don't like it if it's seen as a means to an end, and that at some point the practice will result in the performance. The same thing with Zen practice. It's a word we fall into, and I wish I had a better word. Sitting on the cushion is just living. Practicing law is just 'lawing.' But I don't have a better word."

---

84 Trial Guides, 2018.

He tells me that since the pandemic he has hosted a regular Zen Lawyer Work Retreat on Zoom. The idea came to him during a sesshin. "In sesshin we have sitting and walking meditation – zazen and *kinhin* (walking meditation) – but we also have *samu* or work practice. Raking the leaves and picking up the sticks, washing the dishes and toilets; whatever your work assignment is that day. And that's traditional Zen – chop the carrots.[85] The way I understand it, we sit on the mat, and then we take that awareness to walking, and then we take that awareness to chopping, and then we take that awareness to much more challenging situations like interacting with people. So I thought, 'What about law practice as samu?' So a few lawyers get together – usually a handful – and we sit two twenty-minute sessions of zazen; we do a kinhin in between; we do some quick stretching. And then I'll ring the bell, and the work practice begins. We're actually all witnessing each other. We're not going to go check our emails; we're not going to go on Facebook. For me, maybe it's a particular brief I'm working on or an opening statement. Other people have different things they're working on. And we set an intention that this work we're doing is to alleviate suffering and to do good in the world, that we keep a compassionate mind, and that we do that work together. We do that for several hours. And the people who do it have found it very powerful to have that kind of deep concentration with that framing of doing good in the world."

Sally ZenKa Metcalf

Sally ZenKa Metcalf is a *sensei* at Genjo Marinello's[86] Chobo-ji in Seattle. She points out that the title is largely honorific, explaining that Genjo Osho, as she refers to him, awards it as a way of "acknowledging certain people in this sangha who are not ordained but who have done forty sesshin and at least ten years of practice. Sensei are active helping the community, have held all temple posts, and are sometimes asked to lead sits or give informal Dharma talks."

For Sally, the practice is very much the development and embodiment of karuna/compassion. "What use is our practice if it's not applicable in our lives? Zen talk overflows with profundities. My reaction often is, 'That's great, but what does it mean on the ground running in my life?' Ultimately, compassion is how we hold each other in care, day-in and day-out. Over recent years homelessness has grown in Seattle. Everywhere, hungry faces looked out from rain-soaked tents, beat-up camper vans, and even from cardboard boxes

---

85   He's alluding to the story of Layman Pang, an 8th century Chan practitioner famed for declaring, "I exercise occult and subtle power. How miraculous! How wondrous! Hauling water and carrying wood!"

86   Cf. *Zen Conversations,* Pp. 102-03; 143.

cobbled together. Yet our big Zen kitchen stood unused except for occasional sesshin. Then we started cooking a hundred meals a month for the people in the camps. Spooning up steaming helpings of tasty vegetarian love to our homeless neighbors, we learned their names at last.

"I used to have a little blue boat and took it rowing on Eagle Harbor, my old dog in the bow. Even a little rowboat leaves a wake. What kind of wake does my life make? I live a rather small life in contrast to someone like the Dalai Lama who touches millions of people. I do my best to connect warmly with people through my job for a non-profit that fosters safe and healthy families, and in nearby stores, and on neighborhood walks. My temple time goes to sweeping, laundry and dishes, and weeding the garden, all to make things good for the beings who come here. And there is my much-loved sangha. I greet people among the flowers or at the zendo door, doing my best to learn their names and to listen deeply to them: the guy who welds airplane parts, the landscaper, the capoeira fan, the guy who can fix anything, the mom with two little boys on her mind. Their stresses. Their hopes. Their questions. It's an intimate life."

Before ZenKa took up Zen practice, she had been deeply affected by a program called A Course in Miracles based on a 1976 book by Helen Schucman and Bill Thetford.

"My three greatest takeaways from the course were, first, the practice of forgiveness, seeing all hurt and harm as 'a compassionate device to liberate me from my own egoistic delusions and attachments,' as is expressed so beautifully in Torei Zenji's *Bodhisattva's Vow*.[87] It's wonderful how my Zen and Christian backgrounds interweave. Second, listening to the still small voice within, which Genjo Roshi calls the voice of our True Nature. He once told me if we can follow that voice, we have no need of him, nor any book, nor any teacher. And third, the prayer 'I am here only to be truly helpful' which calls me back to myself again and again.

"A little boat's wake has a gentle lift, like lifting hearts. That's how I want to move through my life, leaving everyone a little lighter and more at ease in the lift of our mutual joy. To do this with others starts with me. The joyful rise is missed if I'm preoccupied, fearful, blaming. Whatever gets in the way of loving care becomes kindling for my zazen furnace, craziness burned to ash. Our founding abbot, Genki Takabayashi Roshi, spoke just a little English. His shorthand for our first Great Bodhisattva Vow was, 'To care for all beings, everywhere, always.' That includes me, you, the garden birds, flowers, bugs, stones, breeze, stars. Hearts lifting together. I don't want to miss a single chance to care."

---

87 See Appendix 4.

Jissai Prince-Cherry

Jissai Prince-Cherry is the Group Leader and a Priest at the Louisville Zen Center. On their website, Bodhin Kjolhede of the Rochester Zen Center is identified as the Guiding Teacher. I ask her what the difference between the two roles is.

"A Group Leader is a boots-on-the-ground person that helps make things happen locally. So, because I'm in Louisville and the teacher is in Rochester – ten hours away – I make sure sittings and other events happen here, and I'm also authorized to do some instructing. But locals who really want to connect with the teacher and do longer retreats, they need to go to Rochester to work with Roshi directly.

"We use my home for most of our sittings, for our retreats, for when guest teachers visit us. I raised my family here, and I'm the only one left living here. It just made sense to use this house in some useful way other than there being the echo of me talking to the cat. So this is where most of the things happen with the Louisville Zen Center."

She had grown up in High Point, North Carolina. "It was very, very segregated. I grew up in a Black neighborhood. My parents owned their home, but we lived across the street from a sprawling housing project. People in the projects thought we were rich because we had our own house. But we were 'house poor.' Most of my parents' income went towards paying the bills for the house. We were just as poor as my friends in the projects were. Not only was my hometown segregated, it was racially hostile with few meaningful job opportunities for Black people, so I left when I was 18 and went into the Air Force. My older brother had gone into the Marines, and I was like, 'I'm gettin' out of here, too!' And I think the Air Force, the military, and those experiences opened the door in allowing me to practice Zen. Opened up that possibility in my mind and my heart."

I ask how it did that.

"The military lifestyle. Everything was standardized. We wore uniforms. Everything was uniform. But even within all of that structure, there was so much freedom. It's like when one of my sons, before he learned to swim, he would hold onto the side of the pool for support. Because he didn't know how to swim, he could only circle the perimeter of the pool holding onto the sides. Then when he learned to swim, he could go anywhere in the pool – on top of the water, under the water, the shallow end, the deep end – but it was still a pool. He was still bound by the swimming pool. But he had all this freedom in it. That's how I felt in the military. There was this firm, stable structure that let me find out what I liked, what I didn't like, who I was. I was able to explore with the help of the supports."

When she discovered Zen, she found that it provided a similar support structure for self-examination.

"Zen practice has opened me up. It has allowed me to see my own contributions to my pain and to others' pain, and how there's really not much of a difference between the two. And to have the courage to face that and to work with that. Even just to see it. You know, it's not so much that there needs to be something done, that I need to roll up my sleeves and get in there and open up the hood and start tinkering around with things. Just the act of seeing ... just the act of seeing what's there. It's like when I was in the Air Force, I was doing some training at an Air Force base in Biloxi, Mississippi, and the dormitory I was in was infested with roaches. I don't know if you know Mississippi roaches, but I never met roaches like this. They *fly*! But just turning on the light – you know – at night, you hear them scurrying around and flying, and as soon as the light gets turned on, you can really see what's there. And that's what practice is like for me. It's like turning on the light and seeing the roaches and seeing the mess they've left behind. And somehow seeing it, it's like it resolves it in some way. I'm no longer blind to the pain I'm causing, not just blindly reacting. And when some people see this stuff in themselves, they get scared; they think that the practice is making them worse. But it's not true. And I tell them," – speaking gently – "'No, it's not making things worse. It's just now you can see what's already there. What's been there all along.'"

I ask how it does this. She uses a comparison that I have heard other people associated with the Rochester Center use.

"The example that I absolutely love is the snow-globe. When we are engaged in our lives, thoughts whirling about – most of them, of course, about ourselves – it's like shaking that snow-globe and the snow swirling, and, in this practice, we just put the snow-globe down, and the snow settles, and we can see the scenery inside the snow-globe. We see what's there that we couldn't see before. That's what this practice does. It allows things to settle so we can see what we're made of."

We see the ways in which "we're causing pain or how we're not relating well to one another. We see what gets in the way. We see where we're stuck. This practice is like ... Well, it is; it's intimacy. Intimacy with our own lives, intimacy with our own stuff, with what gets in the way in our relationships with others, our relationship with our own minds and our own hearts. And when the snow settles and we're seeing into the snow-globe, we're simply seeing what's there already."

By itself, however, clarity is insufficient, which is why there are the examples of people with decades of practice whose behavior still falls short.

"You can kick the dog mindfully," Jissai says. "Or beat your wife with full awareness. Completely mindfully, knowing exactly what you're doing. That's why we also have the Precepts to help guide our behavior. For me the Precepts not only show me how to be, they also describe how I already am. For instance, one of the Precepts says, 'I resolve not to kill but to cherish all life.' When I'm not killing in any of the many ways that we take life, I am cherishing life. I don't have to do anything special to cherish life. Cherishing life is already there fully formed underneath not killing. It's like how the chants are already there fully formed within me. It's just I don't have the words to express it myself."

She found one chant in particular, *Affirming Faith in Mind* – attributed to the traditional Third Patriarch of Chan, Jianzhi Sengcan[88] – so meaningful that she copied it and carried it in her wallet.

"It always spoke to me, spoke to my condition. With it in my wallet, whenever I found myself in some state – usually some state of upsetness – I'd pull out *Affirming Faith in Mind* and start reading anywhere, and it would diagnose what was going on in me, which was usually some self-centered thing. Not only would it diagnose where I was stuck, it would point me in a direction that could get me unstuck. It always felt like that chant was expressing something I knew already, but in the heat of the moment, I didn't know I knew!"

"What does Zen do for people?"

She reflects before answering. "I remember hearing this teacher talking about the Four Bodhisattva Vows.[89] I don't remember his name, but what he said was the First Vow is accomplished through the Second Vow, which is accomplished through the Third Vow, which is accomplished through the Fourth Vow. What a relief! I only had one impossible vow to deal with instead of four! So that Fourth Vow was the most important one for me. It was my focus. 'The Great Way of Buddha, I vow to attain.' That's what I see Zen doing for people. Showing people how to evolve into who and what they already are. That's what I see happening within me, too. I'm becoming more myself. That's why the process of meditation is so attractive to me because it feels like every day I'm becoming more and more who I already am. And I see that with other people, too. They become more and more themselves and are comfortable with being themselves. And they become more and more okay with other people not being okay with them being themselves. Being okay with themselves and being okay with other people being themselves is a beautiful thing."

---

88   See Appendix 3.

89   See Appendix 2.

6
Vows and Precepts

The Four Bodhisattva vows are common to all forms of Zen. They are recited at the end of formal periods of zazen and multiple times during retreats. I initially encountered them at the first sesshin I attended in Montreal. The daily chants and recitations were alternately in French or English, so the first time I heard the Vows they were in a language I don't speak or understand.

> Tous les êtres innombrables,
> > je fais voeu de libérer.
> Les passions aveugles et sans fin,
> > je fais voeu de vaincre.
> Les barrières infinies du Dharma,
> > je fais voeu de franchir.
> La grande Voie du Bouddha,
> > je fais voeu de l'atteindre.

Like many Anglophones, I find the sound of spoken French pleasing and a little exotic. I am also old enough to remember when Catholic masses were recited in Latin. The experience was similar. It was like listening to music that is enjoyable, even soothing, but meaningless.

On the second day of the sesshin, the recitations were in English, and the joke I frequently make is that the Vows made as little sense in English as they had in French.

> All beings, without number,
> > I vow to liberate.
> Endless blind passions,
> > I vow to uproot.
> Dharma gates, beyond measure,
> > I vow to penetrate.
> The Great Way of Buddha,
> > I vow to attain.

One of the things I admired about Zen was its practicality. But, realistically, how could one even begin to address such an agenda? In a way, discovering how to interpret those vows is a koan which each practitioner must resolve on their own.

Judy Roitman

"Every morning practice starts with the Four Great Vows," Judy Roitman informs me. "Every retreat starts with the Four Great Vows, and every day of a retreat ends with the Four Great Vows. Everyone recites these vows. And, you know, Chinese has no pronouns. Most American and Japanese schools translate it as 'I' – '*I* vow' – but we translate it as 'we.' 'Sentient beings are numberless; we vow to save them all.'"

"How literally do you take that vow?" I ask.

"It's a direction. So – like I said – we say the Four Great Vows a lot, and when I started practicing, I was very bothered by this. I had been practicing maybe for a month or two, and I remember going to see Dyan Eagles. She was one of the founding members of the Cambridge Zen Center, and she's absolutely wonderful. And she's this tiny little woman, even shorter than I am. And I remember saying to her, 'Dyan, this doesn't make sense to me. How can I vow to save all beings?' And she stood on tiptoe and kind of tapped me on the head and said, 'Don't worry. You'll get it.'" Judy laughs. "So that's kind of the spirit. Yeah, you don't know what this is. You're gonna find out."

"So are they just words we say without thinking about the meaning of them?" I persist. "Like being in grade school and – hand over heart – reciting the Pledge of Allegiance even though you probably don't know what the words 'pledge' or 'allegiance' mean?"

"They're things we say to remind us what our job is. If you don't say it, then you don't know what your job is. It's pointing out your direction. This is the direction of this practice."

John Pulleyn

"I usually tell people, the easiest way to get a handle on understanding the Four Vows is to see them as aspirational," John Pulleyn tells me. "There is a direction, and the actual saving all sentient beings is very far down that road beyond any conception that we could have. I mean, how do you save all beings? They keep making more. But what you're saying is, 'That's the direction I'm going in.'

"I love the story where there's some guy walking down the beach, and there's all these starfish that have washed up; they're all stranded. So he's throwing them back, and somebody says, 'What's the point? You can never save them all.' 'Yeah. But I can save this one.'"

"So what are you saving them from?" I ask. "'Beings without number, I vow to liberate.' What are you liberating them from?"

"You're vowing to liberate yourself too. From delusion. You know, the Buddha said at his enlightenment, 'All beings are whole and complete – lacking nothing – but because their minds are turned upside down by delusive thinking, they fail to perceive this.' So you're helping yourself and everyone to be able to see."

Rafe Martin

"Okay. Here's the great thing about Zen Buddhism," Rafe Martin says in an excited tone. "Our vows are for 'All beings.' It doesn't mean just you or people like you. It doesn't even mean just human beings. It means dogs, cats, trees, rivers, mountains, clams, bugs. Everything is a being. Which is rather daunting. What could such an immense vow – 'the many beings are numberless; I vow to save them all' – possibly mean? How can *I* save them all when it so often seems I can barely save myself?

"So, first of all, I think it's a tremendous wish, a tremendous aspiration to see every living being freed from self-torment, freed from despair, freed from anguish and anxiety, freed from the terror of death, freed, indeed, from the self-centeredness which traps them into pre-prepared boxes and ends up causing so much harm. Every time we catch ourselves in one of those isolating, judging kinds of mental conditions, we realize something's off, that we've hurt and limited others and ourselves. So if you've ever felt that, wouldn't it be great to move your life in the direction of doing something about it in a way that doesn't harm yourself or add to your guilt?

"To start with, think of it as a desire – a deep-seated desire in our being – to be of benefit to *all* living beings. That's a wonderful feeling to start with. There's something deeply human about it and, I think, deeply freeing to acknowledge it. Like it's already there at our core. And then to realize that there's a direct and straightforward way to begin doing it! 'Greed, anger, ignorance, arise endlessly; I vow to abandon them.' If you want to actualize that great vow to save or free all beings, first of all we have to see what's standing in its way. If I pay attention, let's say by doing zazen, I begin to see that greed, anger, and ignorance arise in my own mind, over and over, endlessly! The core of that is my own self-centeredness, my habitual unconscious commitment to viewing pretty much everything through the lens of 'me, myself and I.' Simply recognizing this will not in itself get rid of these Three Poisons. And Zen practice is not about suppressing or forcefully trying to stop it. You can't. But if I can see such self-oriented thoughts arise and, by paying attention to the practice rather than continuing to indulge or latch onto them, if, in short, I don't build my nest on them, they pass. Then, in time, I might not take them so seriously, not act on them in the same way I used to. I'm starting to put myself in touch with what is beyond or is more than myself. I start to care about what's out there and, in little ordinary ways, begin to naturally participate in building a better, more compassionate world. At the same time, I'm freeing myself from limiting, self-oriented habits of mind. Which, in turn, further creates possibilities of opening to something that, for lack of a better word, is larger or more intimate, and so, more real, than constant thoughts of myself.

"Then 'Dharma gates are countless; I vow to wake to them all' means to wake to the squeak of the toilet seat, the taste of this tea, this angry word from this guy who gives me the finger as I'm driving past him, all of which have the potential to lead me to greater awareness of who and what I am right now, here in this present moment. Not in my head, not drifting, not peering out through the old habitual sense of myself. Everything has the potential to be a Dharma gate, opening us more deeply into life, helping us become more deeply – which means more selflessly – present. Then again, in our tradition we also have several thousand koans – if we include the checking questions and various Dharma points – to help us explore the reality of our being in the world. So it might be helpful right from the start to *vow* to wake to them all. When the mountain seems too steep to climb, that vow can help us persevere.

"Finally, 'The Buddha Way is unattainable,' because fundamentally it's nothing at all. When you really look into it, there's nothing there. But to embody that 'nothing' which is – strangely – filled with compassionate interest in *everything*, to embody that in all that you do ... You can't own it. You can't grab it. You can't become what you already *are*. The Buddha way can't be *attained*. How can you attain what you already *are*? It can't be held, can't be grasped. But you can embody it. You can make it the foundation of how you interact with yourself and the world. You can live from it, embodying it in all you do. Which, given our ancient self-oriented habits, can take a *looong* time to actually be able to do. So, we vow to do it because it will take effort and time.

"So these vows point out a path of aspiration, of what we aim to one day accomplish in the loftiest possible sense. But to start, we simply practice reciting them, being aware of them as guides, letting them help us see how things might truly, wisely be in our lives. And we try to live up to them just as we are, where we are."

Karin Kempe

Karin Kempe's father had been among the Jewish children evacuated from Germany early in the Nazi regime. His parents went to South America while he and his sister were separately sent to Britain. Eventually the family reunited in the United States where he studied medicine and became a virologist.

"He worked on the eradication of smallpox. And much later, as the Chair of the Department of Pediatrics at CU Medical School, he and a colleague, Brandt Steele, identified and studied what they called at the time the 'Battered-Child Syndrome,' to describe kids who had been abused by their parents. Their work transformed the landscape of medicine, psychotherapy, social services and resulted in legislation and programs to protect children and heal families.

"Like most second-generation survivors – although I didn't realize all of this until much later in my life – I had my share of survivor guilt. My dad felt that it was not enough to just live your life, you had to do something to help others. He was absolutely determined to save these kids, and he wanted me and my four sisters, all of us to do something in the world to make a difference. This was a heavy burden, and I felt a great deal of angst as a child, although I didn't understand it for a long time. And it's interesting that although I decided fairly young that I wasn't Jewish, within a few years of becoming a more adult person – maybe 17 years old – I was drawn to a religion in which the first vow is to save all sentient beings. I think, for me karmically, there was a big relationship between my affinity with Buddhism and my past."

"What does that vow mean to you?" I ask. "To save all sentient beings."

"It means that we align our life, our energy, in a particular way. Sometimes these are called the 'impossible vows' because they're never fully accomplished, but we commit ourselves anyway. We recognize that alignment as an expression of who we are together. You and me. And 'liberate' does not mean that from the outside 'I liberate you,' but rather that because we are not separate, this awakening, this opening, which is the expression of the awake universe – I can't explain it another way – that that is happening simultaneously for us all."

Sarah Bender

People working within Joan Sutherland's Open Source network express the vows as Joan and John Tarrant translated them: "I vow to wake the beings of the world. I vow to set endless heartache to rest. I vow to walk through every wisdom gate. I vow to live the great Buddha way."

"'I vow to wake the beings of the world,'" I repeat to Sarah Bender. "Including the nematodes?"

Sarah laughs. "Yeah, we include those as well. I'm not sure they need any help."

"Waking them from what?"

"Right. So I know some people who say, 'I vow to wake *with*.' That would be an acceptable version to me. But I think that the core understanding of the Bodhisattva Way – which is not just Zen; it's Mahayana – is that there's not truly any individual awakening. There's only the awakening of all of us, the on-going awakening of all of us. And when I make the Bodhisattva Vow to wake the beings of the world, what I'm saying is I'm dedicating my however many lifetimes it is – even if I believe that they are sequential – to this awakening of all of us, understanding that even if I wanted to be awakened and end the cycle that would not be an act of generosity, and without generosity none of us can be awakened." She reflects for a moment, then adds, "You know, today I think we understand all the vows as being words that carry the vow but are not the vow itself."

"The word 'vow' itself is interesting," I suggest. "It's more than a promise; it's more than just, 'I'll think about maybe getting around to doing something.' A 'vow' implies a commitment."

"Total. That's right, and so I think that the commitment happens at the preverbal level. The commitment that we use words to express is not completely expressible in words. So I worry less about the exact words than I used to. I think the vow comes before the words."

Meido Moore

"The Chinese character translated in the first of the Four Vows as 'without number' can be read differently," Meido Moore explains. "It can mean 'innumerable,' 'without number,' sometimes translated as 'infinite.' But it can also be translated as 'without boundaries.' Boundless. So we use the word 'boundless.'

"What's important to me about the Four Vows is not only the surface level meaning, but each of them is also an emptiness teaching, or a teaching pointing directly to our nature. For example, what does it mean to say that sentient beings are boundless? That's an important way to look at that vow. But it doesn't negate the surface meaning of 'I'm vowing to help all beings.'"

"How do you translate the first vow?" I ask.

"'I vow to deliver the boundless sentient beings' or 'Sentient beings are boundless, I vow to liberate them.' Something like that."

"And it means?"

"To use your life not only for yourself, because what we call a 'being' is not bounded or limited like that. It means we resolve to actualize the highest human potential of wisdom and compassion, to see clearly what so-called beings actually are. However long that takes, we are going to do that. It will be freeing for ourselves; it will resolve the questions of our own angst and suffering. But recognizing that these other beings have the same kind of angst and suffering, they are included too. They are encompassed. That is what my life is, what it is for. It's not only I or me."

"What is the role of the Precepts then? In traditional Christianity, for example, it's pretty simple. There are some rules God gave us, and if we don't follow them, he's not going to be pleased about it. What role do the Precepts play in Buddhism?"

"Of course, they're not coming from anyone up above. They're human rules," he says, chuckling. "That's the first thing we have to point out to people if they're not aware of that. Broadly speaking, I could say the Precepts recepts have two really important roles. First, if we are concerned with and encompassing others in this path of awakening and self-refinement that we're engaged in, we have to know how not to harm others as well as ourselves. They're very practical rules. I don't steal because I shouldn't steal; that's your stuff; it's not my stuff. It's a very surface level meaning which is important. At the same time, we can look at each of them again as a more profound teaching pointing to the core realization of Zen. If I, for example, vow not to steal, I also have to say, 'Is it possible to own anything at all? Is it possible to have possession of something?' We have to look at each of those things in a more profound way which nevertheless does not negate the common meanings as practical rules for harmonious living, for not harming others, not harming myself. That's one thing.

"Second, the Precepts also serve as a kind of container or nest for one's meditative practice, for the attainment that one begins to actualize. If we do not have that basic container of regulating our activity, we will not be able, for example, to cultivate the profound samadhi – meditative absorption – that Zen requires. We can experience some profound awakening, but if we don't bring our actions of body, speech, and mind into accord with it, we will not be able to sustain the face of that, and ultimately deepen it.

"So just from the standpoint of individual practice, I have to constantly ask myself: how am I cultivating my Zen path? If I do not have basic rules regulating my behavior, it will be impossible to bring that path to fruition. For example, if I'm constantly intoxicated, if I'm constantly breaking that precept, it doesn't matter how much I sit. My meditation cultivation will not advance sufficiently.

"To me those are the two sides of it. One is really an affirmation of our Bodhisattva commitment to aid and encompass others in our activity. The other is from the standpoint of my own training: the Precepts are one of the foundational supports of samadhi cultivation, the cultivation of meditative absorption. And ultimately the kind of things that are expressed in the Precepts become a very true, spontaneous expression coming out from the experience of awakening, rather than something that is being put on me from the outside."

"Of course," I point out, "there have been some pretty spectacular examples of teachers who didn't abide by the precept not to use intoxicants."

"Yeah. I mean, the first thing is there's a difference between lay people and ordained people, traditionally, back to the beginning of Buddhism. For example, the precept against sexual misconduct is quite different for someone who's a celibate monastic. We have to recognize that difference. In Japanese Zen, that is not quite as crucial because we do not use the full Vinaya.[90] We ordain using Bodhisattva Precepts.[91] But that being said, every Buddhist tradition has a way of using and interpreting the Precepts beyond their surface level meaning. I could say that in the Zen view, there could be times when the precept against intoxication means you don't touch it. There could be times when it's fine to touch it. There could be times when if you're drunk but you're aware you're drunk, you haven't broken the precept. If you're drunk and have committed unskillful behaviors while you're drunk, that's the real breaking of the precept. We can look at it in all those various ways.

"Again, it all comes back to 'How do I accomplish the aim of the Zen path?' It's not an orthoprax tradition in the way some others can be. There's no inherent purity or impurity attached to these things. We're looking at all things always skillfully from the standpoint of how they support or hinder the recognition of my nature, and the integration and embodiment of that realization seamlessly in activity, which ultimately is the only true, living Dharma. Within that, there can be a lot of flexibility. And I think that's what's challenging and sometimes frustrating for people about the Buddhist Precepts. They're contextual. Ultimately the responsibility is on the person, not an authority telling us what we should or shouldn't do. We have to learn how to skillfully use these things as tools, rather than be used by them. That's a very creative process, a very wonderful practice. It's also very difficult and frustrating for people who might prefer to just be told what's right, what's wrong, and not have to think about it."

---

90 The part of the traditional Buddhist canon which focuses on rules of behavior for monastics. The number of regulations can vary, but in general there are 253 rules governing men and another 95 – for a total of 348 – rules for women.

91 See Appendix 1.

Debra Seido Martin

Kyogen Carlson taught Seido Martin that the Zen path "distills down to zazen and Precepts. Zazen is the insight, and Precepts are the way that insight moves through the world. And if we take up either one, it requires realization of the other. There's no way to sit zazen and receive the direct reflection on how one is being in the world without bumping into the Precepts. These two are thoroughly integrated. Many people are thankful for the Precepts as a guide to how to face this incredibly troubled world with so much coming at them, about what we should do here and there.

"Each aspect of the Precepts holds all the other aspects. If we pick up the Three Pure Precepts – cease from harm, do good and do good for others, and so on – that's the whole sixteen. The motion of taking refuge in something other than the small self-run show is an entry way into zazen. There's no way to have one without the other. Ultimately, you cannot sit zazen without Precepts. It would be like saying, 'I'm going to do zazen with just the left side of my body but not the right side of my body.'"

"Unfortunately, that's just not the case," I point out. "The history of Zen in North America is littered with examples of people who clearly had little respect for the Precepts."

"I know."

"So how do you explain that?"

"Time to grow up, everybody. We can leave the naïve romantic chapter of Zen and become adults together. My teacher was very humble about the expectations when I confronted him about the failings of Jiyu Kennett, Maezumi, and so many others. As a woman new to practice, I was especially shocked when I first heard of male teachers' sexual abuse of their female students. As an incredibly trusting new student, that I could be taken advantage of by someone in authority whom I trusted seemed awful. We have had much time to learn from this first generation, and we can now be adults. We can take responsibility for our own discernment and call out transgression when we see it. I wouldn't say that teachers who transgressed had no respect for the Precepts; I think they were blind to their own shadow sides and were left unchecked by an undeveloped institution around them. Kyogen said there were no guarantees as to the outcome of this practice for anyone. He was humble and said, 'You know what? I've come to find out after thirty years of teaching that Zen *inclines* us towards wisdom, and it *inclines* toward compassion.' That's it. For everybody.

"And I didn't say you couldn't *break* the Precepts. I said you couldn't do zazen without the *presence* of the Precepts. When you break them, that is a moment of delusion. Keeping them, a moment of enlightenment. When you're doing zazen and you break the Precepts, that is a natural part of your practice. We atone. We move forward. If we think zazen guarantees that we keep them all the time, that's a delusion for sure.

"What I'm saying is you cannot ignore that part of it. I know it's been attempted. That's why in a secular meditation practice the Precepts are often dropped. But you can't deepen your practice and not come into contact with the way you're behaving in the world. Not if you are in touch with a teacher and a sangha."

Seiso Paul Cooper

For Seiso Cooper, the first vow poses a question. "Each moment we have an encounter, how are we going to relate to that encounter? Are we going to relate mindfully or mindlessly? Are we going to relate to it responsively or reactively? To put it in a doctrinal position, we say are we going to relate to it from the Three Poisons of ignorance, attachment, and aversion or from prajna – wisdom – and compassion?"

"Where do the Precepts fit into in all this?"

"They're guides to keep us on the road. It's like getting on a highway where it says, 'Left lane, Montreal; right lane, Vermont.' Or 'Speed limit here 35 miles an hour.' It kind of keeps us on the road."

"Some of those signs are enforceable regulations," I point out. "The 35 miles an hour is different from 'stay in the left lane to get to Montreal.'"

"Yeah, some of them are enforceable regulations, but, for the most part, they're guides. If you go in the left lane, you'll be going over the George Washington Bridge; if you go in the right lane, you'll go to the Palisades Interstate Parkway. So it's your choice. Because I notice when I slip on a precept, it's going to affect my practice. Let's say I spoke harshly to someone, and then afterwards I regret it. And now I'm sitting in zazen. That's going to come up. It's going to affect my practice. So, again, all of this is geared towards practice. You're not going to be condemned to Hell if you go over the George Washington Bridge when you thought you wanted to go on the Palisades Interstate Parkway. It's not like that."

"But you are going to have to work your way back around again."

"You start all over. What I tell people, just come back to the basic fact of sitting."

Hogen Bays

Hogen Bays asserts that anyone "who comes and practices seriously – anyone who picks up the Dharma in earnest – first must learn the tools, the methods, which will help them become calm and embodied. Next, they must find an approach to life that is based not on cultural myths but in the reality of the most basic teaching of the Dharma: change, impermanence, flow, *annica*. With genuine understanding of flow, we recognize that the best way to respond to the everchanging circumstances of our lives is to follow the Precepts. The Precepts are about oneness and responsiveness. Someone who espouses, lives, and talks about the Precepts says, in effect, 'I will not be divisive. I will stay connected. I will encourage healthy relationships.' Living in this way is to recognize the inclusive nature of mind. To live and embody this understanding impacts our life completely."

Jissai Prince-Cherry

"There seem to be many different ways of understanding the First Bodhisattva Vow," Jissai Prince-Cherry tells me. "'All beings without number I vow to liberate' is how we put it at the Zen Center. One way I express it to folks is that my youngest son, he's now 32, but when I dream about him, he's still six or seven years old. And he tells me sometimes I treat him like he's still six or seven years old. And when me and my siblings get together, we're all in our 50s, we kind of ... we don't let each other grow up. We fall back into relating to each other the way we did when we were kids. But when we do that, we're not letting the others be who they are right now because we aren't free. So that's one way of understanding the First Bodhisattva Vow. Allowing oneself and others to be who and what they are in this moment."

Erin Joen Dempsey

Joen Dempsey says something similar. "The first thing that comes to mind is that I will liberate all beings from myself. The buck stops here with karma and my past history and suffering. It stops here. So that's one thing that resonates with me, to vow to free all beings from me, from my desires, my preferences."

Michael Leizerman

"We talked about this when I took the vows in '94," Michael Leizerman reflects. "We studied each of the vows individually, and it was 'strive.' You know?

'I *strive* to free all beings.' To me, there's something in the striving. It doesn't matter if it's attainable. I guess we could argue if it is attainable – the freeing of all beings – but the intention, I think, is important. And 'freeing.' When I consider the language, that sounds condescending. Who am I to 'free?' So it comes back to me as 'reduce suffering, do good, actualize good for others.'"

"And, of course, there's also the question of freeing from what?" I point out.

"At the temple we do something called sangha circles where we get together in groups without our teacher and discuss whatever the topic is, and recently the topic was the Four Noble Truths. And it was helpful to me to look at the translation. We started with 'life is dukkha' or 'there is dukkha.' But translating 'dukkha' as 'suffering' is a little problematic, so we've been translating it as 'clinging.' And this is in keeping with my way of thinking in the world. So if you were to ask me, 'What are we striving to free beings from?' my best understanding would be 'from clinging.'"

"Our clinging or theirs?"

"Both. And from the stories in our minds. This goes along with lawyering really well. When we meet people, we meet the stories in our minds. A lot of it – not all of it – but the freeing of clinging is freeing us from the ways things 'are supposed to be' and recognizing that we have a preconceived notion of somebody is part of that."

"Let me see if I've got this: we can have an idea of what somebody's like. So, I call you up on Skype, and as I do so, I've got this idea about you. 'He's a lawyer. He calls himself a JewBu. He lives in Ohio, for god's sake!' All these things pass through my mind before you say a word. So part of the striving is to free you from my notions of who or what you are?"

"To be aware of it. I think it's important to be aware of where someone comes from or what your prior interactions are. But what's more important is how we are now. So maybe my wife says about something, 'I don't like that.' And now it's in my mind. 'She doesn't like that.' Well, maybe it was just a passing thing. That day she didn't like it, but normally she does. Or a better example: Recently, my oldest son has had some issues. And there was a point where he was very angry, and I was ready to just cut him off. But then," he chuckles, "there's my practice, my Zen vows. It's a practice of trying to bring awareness to the moment and say" – he sighs deliberately – "'Wait. I need to meet him how he is today and give him the benefit of the doubt.' So I had thought, 'I am going to say, "No." It doesn't matter what he says, I'm going to say "No"' because I was attached to having to be strong or whatever I think a father is supposed to be and say, 'No.' But then upon reflection and reflecting back with my wife and other son, 'So wait. I'm going to meet you new. In the moment.' It allowed all that to wash away, and I met him in a place of really deep compassion. And it's had this incredible effect. So here's someone I've known his whole life – know extremely well – and the son I think of from ten years old, twenty years old, even from yesterday, isn't necessarily the son I'm meeting now. Just to have an awareness of that, I think, helps reduce suffering and does good things."

Donna Kowal

Donna Kowal, along with John Pulleyn, is co-director of the Rochester Zen Center. When I spoke with her in 2021, she was then Head of Zendo at the Center's retreat facility located at Chapin Mill, where I once practiced Tai Chi Chuan beside Philip Kapleau's grave. Donna has also trained in Tai Chi, as well as Kung Fu and Qigong, disciplines which eventually led her – in an indirect manner – to Zen practice.

"The reason I took up Kung Fu is that I wanted to learn how to fight in the wake of an assault. I was living in Pittsburgh, and I was the victim of a random physical assault that was incredibly traumatizing on many levels. I was hanging out with friends in a club. There was a band playing and a lot of people there. All of the sudden a woman came through the crowd and choked me. Out of nowhere. It turned out she had been discharged from a psychiatric hospital the day before. What really stuck with me was how I didn't fight back. I just froze. If not for the quick response of the people around me, it might have turned out differently. That's why I started studying martial arts."

Tai Chi, she tells me, is a form of meditation in motion as well as a martial art. I don't disagree. "It's very intensive physical training, and it requires you to be fully present. At around the same time I was studying Tai Chi, there was this new vegetarian café that opened in town, and I went to check it out and got to know the owner. I started talking to her, telling her about Tai Chi and Qigong, and then she tells me, 'Oh, you would like the Zen Center.' And I said, 'What's that?' And it turned out she was an early member of the Rochester Zen Center from back in the early '70s. She's like, 'Yeah, they offer workshops.' So I signed up for a workshop.

"It was a powerful experience. After I signed up for the workshop, the Zen Center sent a brochure in the mail. I opened it up and there was a picture of Roshi Bodhin Kjolhede. That was my first time seeing him. I didn't know what a teacher did in the context of Zen, but I immediately felt like there's something here, something I've been looking for. And when I walked into the main entrance, it immediately hit me that this place is for me. This was before the workshop had even started.

"For me the Four Vows are about seeing everyone you come upon as a person on the Path. We're all finding our way, to one degree or another.

I think of the bumper sticker that Roshi Kjolhede used to have on his car: 'Mean people are suffering.' When we encounter so-called 'difficult people,' how can we see them as people on the Path just like us? It all comes down to our attention in any given moment. When we're with others, where is our mind in that moment? Are we caught up in judgments, or is our attention split between being with them and doing something else? Are we looking over their shoulder, perhaps at the person across the room, or are we fully with them? It comes down to each moment throughout the day. When you're in the grocery store and you're at the checkout line, just being there with the person in front of you.

"We can get these ideas in our head about other people, not just random strangers but people in our lives, family members, friends, co-workers. And we can get locked onto some idea about them, not seeing the person right before us and also not allowing them to change. But – yeah – we all change. We are change."

James Córdova

"There's just the mystery of it," James Córdova muses. "What does it mean to save all beings, to take up a vow that in some ways is insurmountable, that is so large? What I tell my students is as you ... as *I* encounter whatever it is, my own grief, my own fear, my own sense of wishing it were otherwise, my capacity to experience that deeply, to experience that intimately, to have it, to hold it, to carry it with some kindness, to know that it is not separate from any other aspect of my experience, if I can be with this, if I can be with my sadness, then I can be with your sadness. Right? If I can be with this, then I can carry it for you, carry it with you. So the idea of the vow is that whatever the student is carrying, if you can find a way to not turn away from it, if you can find a way to carry it and to allow it and to hold it with compassion then you're of service in the world. This is how we save all beings.

"I think that turning away is the most poignant part, the most painful part of our suffering. All the ways we try to minimize our contact with, 'I don't want to feel this. I'm distracting myself from it. I'm making it a problem. I'm searching for a solution to it. I'm keeping myself busy' – whatever it is – 'I'm trying to medicate it away in some way.' It's how we enact – behaviorally – aversion. Right? 'I gotta get away from this.' And students and patients come to us with that. Like, 'I want to *not* feel this way anymore. I want to feel this idea of equanimity.' They have an idea that equanimity is like floating in an over-salinated pool drifting peacefully. Right? But equanimity with fear feels like fear. It doesn't feel like peace. So the emotionally counter-intuitive move – which is to turns towards and to make room for and to create a home for – is actually the path to wellness and to wholeness and to be of service in the world."

Kokyo Henkel

Kokyo Henkel tells me, "The classic Bodhisattva Vow from the beginning of Mahayana in India is summarized in these four Bodhisattva Vows which begin with 'Beings are numberless, I vow to save them' and end with 'Buddha's way is unsurpassable, I vow to become it.' And you could say all four vows are different aspects of the same vow.

"As I understand it, the classic Buddhist sense of 'saving all beings' did not, originally, refer to activities like feeding the poor or helping an elderly person across the street. It's not that this kind of thing is at all excluded from the spirit of the Bodhisattva, but, in the vow, the word 'saving' is the Chinese character used to translate *paramita*, which means crossing beings over to the other shore or liberating beings from suffering. The Buddha says the only way to really be liberated from suffering is to realize awakening to reality. So we want to awaken beings to reality, to non-dual emptiness. That's what the vow is pointing to.

"But it's interesting – I think – that in modern times I hear people interpret the vow as something more like social action. That that's what 'saving beings' is. Again, I wouldn't want to exclude that kind of activity; it is an aspect of helping to alleviate suffering, but the original meaning of 'saving beings' was to awaken them. And in order to do that, one has to be quite awake oneself. So in that way the vow reminds one who holds this deepest understanding of the vow that this is the reason one is practicing, to awaken, to liberate all beings. An aspiring bodhisattva has to really practice deeply oneself in order to be able to find skillful ways to do that."

"And the purpose is to diminish suffering?" I ask.

"Yes. For all beings. But the suffering that the Bodhisattva Vow is addressing, I would say – as is the case for Buddhism generally – is existential suffering. Buddha's teachings seem to mostly address the mental anguish we unnecessarily cause ourselves. Of course, if somebody's starving, we're not going to tell them about emptiness. That's not going to be helpful. But the point is not so much to relieve their hunger; first we may need to relieve their hunger so that now they're ready to hear about emptiness. Because they're not actually saved by simply being fed and housed."

Hadrian Abbott

Hadrian Abbot is a member of the sitting group I host in Fredericton, New Brunswick. He is a student of the Rinzai teacher, Shodo Harada,[92] and spent seven months resident in Harada's temple in Japan. Hadrian is a nurse, and, a year after he returned to North America, he spent another six months at Enso House, the hospice associated with Harada's center on Whidbey Island in Washington State. He now works in a methadone clinic where, in addition to his other duties, he offers meditation instruction to clients.

"I've thought about the Four Vows a lot since I started the whole 'See the Buddha in Everybody' practice. Our practice includes others, but how do you incorporate that into your daily practice? With the job I'm doing now, most of my day is listening, and I work with really, really challenging people. We follow the harm-reduction model, so most of my day is spent with the handful of people who have prescriptions to inject Dilaudid. They have a prescription from the doctor. We provide clean drugs, clean space, clean equipment. Most of my job is working with that group. And they are the most damaged of the damaged. All of the women have been raped, assaulted, some of them have been trafficked. Everybody's been in jail. Pretty much everybody had an abusive childhood; some are perpetuating the abuse. Some have mental health issues. Most have co-morbidities with the health issues they are dealing with. And the challenge becomes, how do you work with this group? And how do you apply, 'Sentient beings are numberless; I vow to liberate them' when some days it takes a lot of energy to stay calm and stay focused. The solution I've found is simply listening. Not being absent but trying to be present when people talk to me. Unless somebody asks, I rarely offer advice. Which leads to the next challenge. A lot of the people I work with are suspicious of authority. They have low or almost no self-worth. Working out when someone is actually saying 'I need help' is a challenge some days. If people are open enough, you can spot windows. I know them well enough, seeing them four times a week, I can tell when somebody's off. The lives that they lead ... I see a small fraction of their day. It's a challenge. I enjoy the work, but it's really making me rethink my practice."

"In what way?"

"It's going back to the very simple thing, being present in the now."

"I wonder if this effort to be present to the people you work with isn't an attitude you would have developed regardless of whether you were a Zen practitioner or not, just as a compassionate person."

---

92 See fnt 65, p. 63 above.

"I think probably. Yes. But I think if you make it a point of practice it becomes more focused. For me. Also by listening I've learned some very unflattering things about myself. About control. For a long time, I wrestled with, 'Do we all want control or certainty or both?' In our interactions with self and others. Being judgmental. Anger. Expectations."

"Several people, when I've asked them how they understand that first vow, have said that one thing they are liberating others from is their judgment."

"Exactly! Exactly! It's respect for the other as they are. However they are. And what's in front of you is what's there and what you work with. I mean, we're all judgmental, and sometimes that's good – we all need a certain degree of control – but mostly it's bad. And it's simplified my sitting. More and more I sit and see what comes. Whatever comes comes."

7
Looking Forward

Koun Yamada Roshi, who speculated on the possibility of Zen practice finding a home within Catholic spirituality, was not the only 20th century Japanese teacher to lament the decline of the tradition nor to express hope that it might become grounded in the West. To some degree, that process has taken place. Japanese Zen masters whose teaching lineages can be traced back to the 6th century joke about the possibility of having to re-import Zen from America.

On this continent, Zen as a practice – rather than a literary concept – is barely one hundred years old. It can be dated from two events that occurred in 1922. The first was the establishment of the Zenshuji Soto Mission in Los Angeles. The second was the first public talk by Nyogen Senzaki of the Rinzai tradition. Although he didn't do so in that talk, Senzaki would become the first person to give zazen instruction to non-Japanese students.

During the following one hundred years, Zen emerged first as an intriguing intellectual concept and then as a vigorous spiritual tradition. There was an unprecedented blossoming in the 1960s and '70s, but since the 1980s, the numbers of people drawn to the practice as something more than an inexpensive form of psychotherapy or a relaxation technique has begun to decrease. Ironically, the number of places where people can find Zen instruction has increased.

In Japan, the decline continues precipitously. At the end of 2021, there were only four Soto monasteries with more than ten monks. A decade earlier, there had been a dozen. The majority of Zen priests in Japan have inherited their positions. Most function as administrators of family-run temples and many do not engage in regular personal zazen practice. These are the young clerics Jeff Shore teaches, who are bewildered by Western interest in what they privately consider an archaic tradition. The primary activities at most of these temples are funerals and memorial services.

If Zen continues to fare better in North America and Europe than it has in its homeland, that is due, at least in part, to the fact that it has been adapted to Western conditions. The Zen promoted in places like Honolulu, Maine, or New York today is not the Zen which pioneers like Robert Aitken, Walter

Nowick, and Philip Kapleau encountered in Asia, and that, some suggest, has resulted in an enervation of the tradition.

Dosho Port

The pioneers who brought Zen to North America from Japan were familiar with two models, the temple and the monastery. Monasteries were training institutions for people seeking formation as monks and nuns. Temples served the spiritual needs of householders. The most common form of Zen institution in North America today is neither of these; it is the Zen Center, a uniquely Western construct, a place for lay practice – whether Soto, Rinzai, or Sanbo Zen – with or without a focus on awakening and the integration of awakening in one's life.

Once again Dosho puts the matter in a historical perspective.

"As far as I know, in all the cultures in Asia before the 20th century there was a two-track system where the monastics – men and women living in monasteries – were the specialists, some sub-group of those were really focused on awakening in this lifetime. And then householders, who maybe attended temple services, were generally considered either not interested or not able to put the kind of time and energy into waking up that was necessary. Their contribution was to support the specialists and receive merit for doing so.

"Then with the 20th century, a number of things were happening worldwide, some of them specific to Buddhism, but one is the collapse of monasticism for various reasons. And at the same time, fortunately, lots of householders became interested in contemplative traditions including Zen. And then this new iteration on an old thing developed, the idea of 'neither monk nor householder,' which went back to Saicho.[93]

"When people like Suzuki Roshi and Katagiri Roshi came to California in the mid-20th century, what they started with at Sokoji was a traditional kind of Soto temple. And then all these hippies started coming in who actually wanted to sit. And Suzuki Roshi is, like, 'Yeah. This is it. These are the people who are actually neither monk nor householders.' And so they created this new model for rigorous lay training. And the model caught on. Every place it spread did it a little bit differently, but they all basically were doing serious Zen training for householders. So through the late '70s and '80s, when I was at the Minnesota Zen Center before Katagiri Roshi died, we were doing something like three or four hours a day of practice plus having jobs. Plus eight hours on Saturdays. Plus monthly sesshin. And this was not unusual.

---

93   The century founder of Japanese Tendai Buddhism. Flourished 800 CE.

This was the standard for Zen Centers at the time.

"Of course there were some problems with the model. Marriages. Kids. Careers. So it really pushed what was possible for householders, sometimes too far. In most groups today there's a general kind of gentling due to cultural influences and new cultural values about balance and success in the contemporary economy. So Zen Centers have become less like training centers and more like churches where people come once or twice a week for an hour or two, and that's often all the practice they do. They are still called 'Zen Centers,' premised on the capacity for awakening, and often with a backstory that includes stories of the great awakenings of many of our great ancestors, but almost no Zen Center in the country – there are exceptions – now offers a realistic program where great awakening can happen. Most Zen Centers simply do not offer a program with sufficient intensity for householders to experience the kind of absorption necessary for a kensho as clear as the palm of one's hand, as Hakuin liked to put it.

"Today Soto Centers are basically community centers for progressive people that want to come and do a little meditation and occasionally hear a talk about something that they can use in their lives. If there's a children's program that the kids can attend while they're doing their weekly Zen thing, all the better. There's nothing wrong with all that, of course. But it's not Zen training, and there's nothing in the history of Zen that indicates that that kind of limited practice can actually lead anywhere, except maybe to being a nicer person and a better life next time. Zen in the West has become mostly about well-being rather than the Bodhisattva Vow to get to the ground of being in order to benefit all beings.

"You know, there was this idea fifty years ago that Zen was going to convert the West. No! The West has converted Zen. And it's made Zen – with some exceptions – into a progressive belief system, a condiment for progressive living. The Soto Zen Buddhist Association spends most of their time in training people in progressive causes – which I mostly agree with – but that's what they do, not supporting priests in offering the Buddhadharma as it's traditionally been understood. That's also what their conferences are about. They've become a support organization for people that are doing progressive Buddhist community organizing."

"Well, they do teach meditation," I suggest.

"Mostly what they're teaching is a fuzzy form of mindfulness. They're teaching a version of meditation that's only distinguishable from secular mindfulness in its lack of clear outcomes."

"Are there not other schools which still emphasize awakening and the post-awakening process? The Rinzai people, the Sanbo Zen people."

"To some extent. And they are all facing the same pressures. Levelling downwards. That is the Western culture. To find the easiest way through. So you have peoples' kenshos being verified that usually are only faint intimations. I've met with people that are deep into the koan systems in various traditions and for many of them it's all intimation but not what would be called a classical kensho."

In Dosho's view, there needs to be a re-visioning of the way in which Zen is presented in the West.

Scott Thornton

The Sanbo Zen tradition had arisen as an attempt to re-vision Japanese Zen, and, while it has only had modest impact in Japan, it has played a key role in the dissemination of Zen globally.

"Yamada Ryoun Roshi – the son of Yamada Koun Roshi – really believes that North America is where the future is at for Zen," Scott Thornton tells me. "I think that part of what he hopes for in the West is that Zen will become more like us rather than the old, strict, authoritarian Japanese model. There's still a strict quality at our retreats, but there isn't any shouting; there's no grovelling."

"Prostrations?"

"Well, we do prostrations."

"To idols on an altar?" I ask.

"We are *real* clear about that. That figure is not something other than you. That is you right there. That's your Buddha Nature. I think there's a tension between keeping the Japanese forms because they're beautiful to us, but ... Here's something that happens when people come in. I had this happen just the other night. Guy said, 'Okay. What is this?'" Scott places his hands together, palm to palm, in gassho and bows. "And I said, 'It's a Japanese form that we still use to greet, to show respect, and to center ourselves.' So we keep some things, but we're working on it. At the Maria Kannon Center in Dallas, we still sit on *zafus* and *zabutons*, but we call them cushions and mats. And we still have teisho, but we call it a talk. And we still have dokusan, but we call it Private Interview. So it's trying to get away from Japanese words, at least. It's pretty hard to keep people from doing this." He bows again. "I mean, everybody does that. You don't have to be Zen to do that.

"So there are changes happening, and there is resistance in some quarters. Like Henry Shukman is taking a real journey down the path of mindfulness in his program called 'Original Love.' He uses a lot of guided meditation, and he's kind of encouraging us to guide people in sitting. And there's a thread of me that resists that. 'Just be quiet. You're getting in the way of my meditation.' You know? But people find it helpful. They feel that there's more meat to it that way, I think. Another element is Q & A. We never used to have Q & A. But in the Hindu tradition, there's a kind of shared dokusan they call *satsang*. What it is is students asking teachers questions. So we're doing that. Like an ancient tradition we're bringing back."

Karin Kempe

"I'm not sure any more how many people want to do the whole formal training that I did," Karin Kempe admits. "That's a question for me. I find it a beautiful and transcendent path, an inspiring path. Do others? I don't know. I think that Zen has to adapt to different settings, to different cultures, and has to – in some way – inform how we live. And to the extent that it's able to do that, it will survive. But if it's too rigid – if it's preserved too rigidly – then it won't. But as I said earlier, I think the fundamental insight is not limited to Zen. And I think that insight will survive because it's a human capacity. I mean it's like the little plants that are constantly pushing up here and there through the earth and then grow and flower. It's a human capacity that will survive for sure. Zen? I have no idea. It just turns out I spent my whole life doing this thing I love, but you know?" She laughs briefly and shrugs. "Maybe to no avail."

Jean-Luc Foisy

Jean-Luc Foisy tells me that shortly after Albert Low died, another member of the Montreal Board – Louis Bricault – asked Jean-Luc to accompany him to a retreat facilitated by Jeff Shore in Philadelphia. "And I said, 'Well, you can always ask somebody else.' After working with Albert for 25 years, I was very dedicated to Albert's teaching, I was very dedicated to Albert, period, and to be honest, I was afraid. But Louis insisted, and I said, 'That's fine. I'll go.' And actually I am very happy he insisted because it was a good thing to meet somebody completely different from a personality perspective and from a teaching approach as well. You know, having worked with Albert for so many years, for me, he was the absolute. There was nothing other than that, and nothing was possible other than this approach, this personality, this way of being a Zen teacher and so on. So this kind of opened up a door, I would say and I very much appreciated working with Jeff in the context of that retreat.

"So we invited Jeff to come to Montreal. There was some concern, especially with some long-term members who I think were not able to adjust to the style Jeff had. He was very amiable, very open, not as *autoritaire* as Albert was. It was a completely different style. Yet his involvement was greatly appreciated by most members, and we are inviting him to conduct a retreat once a year in Montreal."

Jeff was also very supportive of the effort that Louis and Jean-Luc would provide in order to support the community. "He said on one occasion that his intention was to help us all going through this transition so that we – among ourselves with our own resources – be self-sufficient. I took that quite seriously and went on doing the workshops for newcomers, the one-on-one and group meeting with members, conducting retreats and doing Dharma talks on occasion."

I mentioned that when I spoke with Shore, we discussed his experience in Montreal. "He suggested that people responded awkwardly when he opened up the teisho to discussion."

"I think you mean no one asked a question. And the simple reason is you know what it is to be conditioned, and we were very much conditioned not to talk in the zendo. In my experience, my heartbeat would double before I would even think about doing that, and I could hardly put my thoughts together. Really, I was paralyzed. It takes time. I keep telling people, 'You need to step out of your comfort zone.' In spite of the difficulty, go for it. You may hardly be able to articulate anything and feel you look stupid. Never mind. At least you will heat-up the ice a little bit. And eventually the ice starts to melt, and you get water so you can move freely, unobstructed. Yes, I can very much appreciate Jeff's surprise, because he worked in a different way.

"One thing that I learned from Jeff – and I thought was very interesting – is that in early Buddhism, it was not like the master talking and the monks listening silently. It was someone talking to the lay people and gathering their input, feedback, impressions, questions. Personally, I prefer working with people in this way. So I conduct group meetings. The participants are invited to select a short text that they propose to the group, and we meditate on its content for a month. We then get together in a small group for one hour, and we share our reflections on its content. The last one we just worked with was the *Dogen Uji*.[94]

"I still feel a very strong connection with Albert and his Dharma. The sensation is very clear: as much as I'm willing to engage, he's there." He smiles. "As simple as that. And it is not only him, but it's the whole line of masters and people … No, no. Let's forget about the term 'masters.' It is the whole line of people who dedicated their lives to this … this … I don't have a name for it. But when you line up with it, you feel a very strong support.

"I am conducting an introduction workshop almost every month now because there is an ongoing demand. We also offer a follow-up workshop

---

94   A document by Dogen included in Philip Kapleau's *The Three Pillars of Zen*.

which is four evenings, each with specific themes in connection with Zen practice. We offer this primarily to participants who have expressed an interest in the practice and are willing to engage in it for three months."

Jean-Luc pauses a moment, then adds, "It will be seven years next January [2023] that Albert passed away, and I am very grateful to all the members of our community for their effort to carry on and support this most precious gift."

Hogen Bays

"We are standing on the shoulders of giants," Hogen Bays tells me. "So to honour those giants, we honour our heritage. How do we recognize that heritage and pass it on? As we study and learn we develop an internal sense of our ancestors, all those people who sweated blood to realize, to touch the great mystery. Knowing our similar aspiration for truth, we feel a resonance with them. Externally, we have the forms of our particular style, the format of our way of practicing Zen. Sitting in rows, chanting, work practice, and face-to-face teaching are all manifestations of our heritage.

"You can't really pass on something like that unless there is a degree of faith, and faith is generated by experience. For example, we go to ski in Whistler, Canada. We come back, and because we have touched the slopes of Canada, even though we no longer see them, we now have faith, based on experience, that Canadian skiing really exists. Having direct experience is part of the cultivation of faith.

"And then I think it's incumbent upon all of us to become familiar with the ancestral teachings so we can point out how those same teachings play out right here, right now. Then, we support this particular style of practice. This is the way we learned. I hope that people who grow up in this environment will cherish it, will appreciate it, and say, 'This is part of the medicine that I too can offer.' I hope that people will go forth and continue that offering. Part of the lineage tradition is generosity, that anything we learn we offer to others. I hope our heirs learn and pass on the flavor of the lineage from which they learned. Will they pass on the exact form? Will they ring the same bells or wear this style of robe? I don't know. But I do know there's a sacredness about stepping into the robes which our ancestors have worn for millennia. So I hope this respect is transmitted.

"Also, part of a mature Zen practitioner is that we have some understanding of the particular karmic nature of our own personality. We begin to realize the ways this one-of-a-kind personality with this particular mind can and cannot express the deep truths of Dharma, of life. Each life is unique. Every person sees the world differently. So as the Dharma is passed through each generation, each generation will indubitably filter and shape it, according to what they see as the needs of their unmatched culture and time. I hope our heirs will be wide enough to flexibly adapt to the needs of changing circumstances and deep enough to know the vertical which does not change."

David Weinstein

John Tarrant's Pacific Zen Institute began experimenting with traditional structures very early.

"John started having one day retreats in peoples' living rooms," David Weinstein remembers, "and from that to having multi-day retreats still in peoples' living rooms, until it got to the point where we were considering renting space to have our retreats. John made it clear that he was not going to do it unless his wife and daughter were at the retreat also, and that we arranged childcare so his wife would have some free time to participate."

"How old was his daughter?"

"This was from the time she was born. She's an adult now, but she very much grew up in retreat. We were doing four seven-day retreats a year, and she was there for every one of them. When John initially made the requirement, I thought, 'This is going to be a burden on everyone. We were already preparing the vegetables and washing the pots and pans and serving the food – we were still very much in the Japanese style at the time – it was one more job someone was going to have to do. There were a couple of blocks of childcare in the morning and in the afternoon, maybe four people a day, a couple of hours each taking care of Seraphina and any other kids who happened to be there.

"It created a culture in which parents with young children could attend retreats and bring their kids. There were three or four families who raised their kids during retreat, which was quite wonderful. It turned out, it was fantastic for the people who were volunteering to take care of the kids. People who were a little stuck one way or another or were perhaps rigid in the way they were practicing couldn't do that with the kids. It was natural, original beginner's mind. We realized, 'Oh my gosh, this isn't a burden, it's an opportunity.' Peoples' practice really blossomed from doing childcare."

Rafe Martin

"My wife, Rose, and I were already married with an eight-week-old child when we first came to Rochester," Rafe Martin recalls, "which was all the way back in 1970. That put us in a totally different realm than most of the other young people who were there back then, all of whom planned on being monks or nuns, which was the only thing anyone knew about Zen at the time. There was as yet no recognition of lay practice as its own profoundly genuine path. So, given our circumstances, we had to find our own way. Eventually Roshi Kapleau and Rose and I became very close. His daughter told us that we and a few others were his family. But, while we were very much a part of the Rochester Zen Center for many years, it became clearer and clearer to me that the style of training there would not be my own. In fact, Roshi Kapleau encouraged me to find my own way. He saw early on that that kind of institutional, semi-monastic residential training was really not what I was about. And I think less and less it's what most people who are practicing and interested in the practice of realization are about. I think family, friendships, affinities, vows that bring us to a certain kind of work, all of these are part of the Bodhisattva Vows, helping us to make our way in this world and to do some good."

It was standard for people at the Rochester Center to begin koan study with Mu. After a while, however, Kapleau had Rafe work with Hakuin's "Single Hand" instead.[95] Resolving that led to his subsequent koan work, and it wasn't until several years later, when he was working with Robert Aitken in Hawaii, that he took up Mu again and resolved it.

"And it was terrific, because I found I didn't need a Zen center, I didn't need all kinds of stuff going on. I would be travelling every day, speaking in schools, libraries, a storytelling festival, and at night I would go to dokusan with Aitken Roshi and in this way went through all his checking questions on Mu. And I realized *that* is lay life; *that* is lay practice. You mature from where and as you are. That is your ground, your path to becoming a grown-up human being. And the whole point of the Bodhisattva in Zen – really, literally it means 'wisdom-being' – is someone who is wisely choosing to mature beyond their own habitual unconscious self-centeredness. So a 'wisdom-being' is simply a growing-up being. And I saw that lay life was the perfect ground for that. It wasn't a lesser form than residential training or monastic practice. It was its own form. It was not only valid but was totally valuable, because you can't hide out in it. You can't run from the realities of your life or evade them. You can't think you're getting something and then not function in life. You've got to function or people couldn't care less what your training is. It's how you treat them. How you interact.

"That all began to get clearer to me, and finally when Danan Henry Roshi ordained me in 2009, he said, 'I'm ordaining you at the same level as a monk or priest, but as a lay person.' So, I'm ordained but as a lay person. Basically, I decided to be me and to teach lay Zen practice as a lay Zen teacher. And that's

---

95 "What is the sound of the single hand?" Often translated as "What is the sound of one hand clapping?"

what I've done. I've stayed small, intimate, non-institutional, non-residential. The test is, 'How's it going in your life?' And that, to me, is what koan practice is about.

"I don't have a lot of feeling for Japanese styles. I don't have a lot of feeling for wearing certain kinds of clothing. I don't have a lot of feeling for a certain kind of protocol. I don't have a feeling for certain formulaic kinds of behaviors. But I do have a very deep feeling that maturing as human beings is why we're here. And I feel very deeply that Zen is one of the more accessible paths – maybe the most accessible path – to growing up as a human being, not just adding more knowledge or more gold stars or feathers to our caps. To me a 'growing-up human being,' means one who is maturing beyond their own habitual self-centeredness. Who knows what's possible in and through such a life? I feel that it's the happiest form of life we can aspire to. And when you get through the clutter, that's what a so-called spiritual path like Zen is about.

"Along these lines, I believe deeply in our complete koan curriculum, the second half of which – the formal koan books coming after the *Blue Cliff Record* – helps rid us of the taint of, 'I've got it!' that can emerge in the first half. There's something more subtle and settled that emerges out of the complete curriculum. So the way I work with students is not that you're necessarily initially going to have some over-powering experience and now you're *enlightened* and you traipse through the subsequent koans. Rather, with a first glimpse, you might just have enough to allow you to start responding appropriately to checking questions on an initial koan. Then, gradually, over years of on-going practice, which means regular dokusan, daily zazen, and periodic sesshin, that initial glimpse widens and deepens, and genuinely self-confirming experiences do happen.

"I like Aitken Roshi's point that while satori implies some total wisdom or transformative insight, kensho means something much humbler, simply 'seeing self-nature.' It gives us enough to start working on realizing non-dual living. But self-confirming realization, real maturity of insight as well as its integration into an ordinary decent life can be many, many years down the road. My faith is that the curriculum will be transformative in the long run if the teacher is accurate and if the student honestly persists.

"I think 50 or 100 years from now, we're going to see many fewer Asian accoutrements. I think that any teachers who might come after me through Endless Path Zendo will have a deeper understanding of intimacy. Aitken Roshi felt that 'intimacy' is the traditional meaning of 'realization' or 'enlightenment.' It's not that you *get* something called enlightenment. Rather you become 'intimate with' everything, without the old habitual clinging to a sense of isolation or separation. Intimacy is where the future of Zen lies. The practice of the Way of the human being is what's important. If the practice helps in that direction, it's deeply useful. If it doesn't, if it simply becomes another self-important thing in itself – something whose forms we sentimentally or authoritatively cling to – then I don't know how much lasting value it will have."

Joshin Byrnes

When Joshin Byrnes tells me there is a residential training program for novice priests at Bread Loaf Mountain, I ask him what they will do once ordained.

"That's a very good question. It's a question we grapple with all the time. We don't know exactly. These are the questions on the table. What is priesthood? Why do it? What does it contribute to anything? What does a priest do? And then there's the way that the Japanese tradition in Soto holds priesthood. In reality, in a sangha like ours, once you take on the identify of even being a novice priest you become, in many ways, like a chaplain or a spiritual care provider because that's what our culture looks to priests to do. And if you're holding a sangha where you're opening up space for people to do deep spiritual exploration, then a priest is looked at as somebody who can give spiritual guidance. And we're talking about what that means.

"In our tradition, the terms 'priest' and 'monastic' have been exchanged with one another at different times. We wonder if we are more New Monastics than we are priests. This is a big question for us at the moment. In fact, I met recently with Eve Marko to talk about some of these things – you know, Bernie Glassman's wife – and she's a lay person. Bernie became a lay person. I'm curious about people who have not taken on priesthood or have let it go."

On the one hand, Joshin tells me what attracted him to Zen was that it was not doctrinal or dogmatic. Then he tells me he took part in up to fifty programs a year when he was working with Joan Halifax at Upaya. I ask what those programs were focused on if it wasn't doctrinal instruction.

"Well, Roshi Joan created what she called a big tent. And I appreciated that a great deal. So sometimes we were studying Buddhism as a religion, and we'd study the primitive Pali Canon texts. So there was this kind of religious foundation to a lot of what we did, but it wasn't all of that. We also did a lot in neuroscience, social science. We did a lot of inner psychological work using the scaffolding of mindfulness. A lot of work on trauma and resiliency. So there were many, many things that I was exposed to there. Catholic priests used to come; we would have rabbis come; we would have Sufis come. You know, one of the modern terms today in society is 'intersectionality,' and I think of my training at Upaya as akin to intersectionality. What does Buddhism have to offer us today? Not as a way to be loyal to Buddhism but as a way to live a fruitful life in the complexity of our contemporary society and contemporary mindsets.

"I think Roshi Joan would say that she's Buddhist. She used to say when we took vows that 'You're taking Buddhist vows.' And this is true in many ways. But I also think there was another aspect to it, which is that Buddhism is a tool for living your life. And just like the Buddha taught, if it works use it, and if it doesn't don't. That's the place I sit with it in many ways. There are some settings in which it is important for me to state that I practice within the religion of Buddhism, and there are other times when it is not useful to state that."

The "New Monasticism" he refers to is a concept developed by lay Christians in Britain during the 1970s and '80s. The material Joshin sends me about it reminds me of D.T. Suzuki's early writing in which he suggested that Zen was a universal concept that could be found in the majority of the world's religions, an insight that transcended any particular cultural matrix. Joshin tells me that's his understanding as well.

"You know, Thomas Merton[96] in *Zen and the Birds of Appetite* says something like, 'Mysticism is to Christianity what Zen is to Buddhism.' There's a relationship, but it's free. Mysticism is free of Christianity in a way as Zen is free of Buddhism. So they come out of these traditions, and they are part of them, but also they are not encompassed completely within the box of Christianity or Buddhism.

"We're not in the culture that provided the philosophical and cultural context within which Buddhism emerged, and I think that's part of the experiment of Buddhism in the West. I think we have to be careful about shoving square Buddhism into round Western frameworks. There's a lot of overlaps. There's a lot that can fit, but there are things that really don't."

"Merton doubted that Western people could actually practice Zen," I mention.

"That's right. And the Dalai Lama has said, 'Maybe you should learn to practice within your own Western context.' Rather than just reject it but explore it deeply."

"So to get a handle on this, is it that in the New Monasticism people are exploring to what extent the kind of activity or study traditionally associated with monastic life can be applied to lay life?"

"I think the whole distinction between lay and monastic gets blurred in New Monasticism and quite intentionally. In some ways it's a funny remnant – isn't it? – that we think only those that have separated themselves from society are capable of reaching high levels of spiritual insight. That is an odd thing, and I think it's a cultural remnant. I would say we should question that assumption.

---

96   A Trappist monk and writer.

Anyone is capable of spiritual insight – profound spiritual insight – and spiritual experience. So what are the structures and systems that allow people to practice rigorously even though they are not living on the outskirts of town or up on top of a mountain or in a cave? I think this is a Zen gift. Can our ordinary daily lives, can washing your bowl be a path to awakening? And if we practice whole-heartedly with whatever we've got, wherever we are, no matter what conditions we place ourselves in, isn't the opportunity of awakening always there? Because Buddha's always there. Your own Buddha Nature is always there.

"So I live a New Monastic life. I have a partner; I have a home. I've had a job. I have children. I have grandchildren. I have to worry about retirement, and I have to pay my electricity bill. So can't I awaken in that context? That's how I view the New Monasticism."

Cynthia Kear

Cynthia Kear is in a peer group along with Joshin and Diane Fitzgerald of Zen DownEast in Pembroke, Maine.[97] Cynthia tells me that the New Monasticism model has influenced the direction in which her Great Spirit Sangha is going. "The group is for people who, like me, are not casual Buddhist practitioners. They attend regularly. They want to study the Precepts. They want to study Buddhism. They want to have jukai. They want to do this more formally, but they don't want to necessarily go to a monastery, or they may not have the time or money. My experience through the various spheres of community that I've been exposed to here in the Bay Area – the Suzuki Roshi lineages – is often somebody has jukai and then what? So I'm working with my sangha to create what we're calling Monks in the Marketplace or Community-Based Practice to help identify and give more structure and clarification to what this practice is all about and what it could be all about.

"The New Monasticism model is about your daily practice, your monthly practice, your annual practice. What is your vow? What is your commitment to sangha? Do you meet regularly with the teacher? What is your commitment to service? And that's where issues like climate chaos and social justice come in. But not exclusively. Because I consider being a good parent being of service to all beings.

"And then I also added a section where I wanted people to focus on 'How do you practice joy?' Because I think these have been some hard years, and there are some hard things going on around us regardless of politics. We need to make an effort to push against 24-hour news cycles. Not to go into denial

---

97   Cf. *Zen Conversations*, pp. 123; 164-68.

but to make sure there is equal opportunity for cultivating and experiencing joy and happiness, freedom and liberation in one's life. That is really, really important.

"So it's kind of an experiment. Everyone in my sangha's pretty excited. I introduced it about a year or so ago. And everybody's created these common 'statements of intention' about being a monk in the marketplace."

"Are there further changes you foresee the people following you are going to have to make in order for Zen to remain viable in North America?"

"I think taking on the issues which I see the Soto Zen Buddhist Association doing. You know, there's an upcoming series of focus groups on Zen, patriarchy, misogyny, that everyone's invited to. Are you a member of SZBA?"

"I am a lay person with no official standing."

"Oh, you are a person of no rank which we venerate. Excellent. So I think with organizations such as SZBA and at individual practice centers there is new programming geared toward DEI – Diversity, Equity, and Inclusion – so I think this is happening. People are moving this way. There was a really interesting thread on the SZBA list mostly by women talking about the reversal of Roe v Wade, what it means, and how we're going to practice with that, and how we're going to help our students – male and female – deal with that in the present tense and going forward.

"For me, I feel that that patriarchal grasp on the practice is loosening up, and there is more appreciation of gender equity. But I think we're going to have a very, very hard time with diversity. You know, this has such deep roots in all the things that are antithetical to African American culture. Right? Zen people tend to be of a certain socio-economic status. So we need to figure out how to be more attractive to people of colour in order to open up the floodgates so the benefit of the teachings of the Dharma can be shared by everybody.

"I think there has to be some focus given to the shift away from monastic training to how do we meet people where they are. And I think this is loosening, but my own practice started when people were absolutely emphatic, 'You can't possibly be transmitting the Dharma unless you have done x number of practice periods monastically.' Right? Where do these people get these dualistic ideas, Rick? I don't know."

Julie Nelson

The website for the Greater Boston Zen Center states that they offer "LGBTQIA+ and POC sitting groups." Given that Zen is intended to guide people to an understanding which all human being have the inherent capacity to experience, I ask Julie Nelson why it is important to have separate opportunities for those communities.

"There is a real difference in the sense in which one can feel secure and relaxed and open if one's been a part of any kind of marginalized community," she explains. "A difference between being in a community in which one is or is potentially marginalized by other people in the group and a group in which you feel that you can let that guard down. So many of the people who are in that group also sit with the regular Tuesday and Saturday and Wednesday sits. I am not in that community, but, having been in a male-dominated profession as a female for years, I'm certainly aware of how the slightest, often inadvertent, comment or bit of structure going on in a group – totally invisible to people dominant in the group – can suddenly remind you that you don't really belong. And I'm afraid I probably put those signals out as well for groups that I'm not a part of. And that's why these groups exist. Although some people may carry it too far. It's not as if we are separate species and can't communicate with each other at all. But simply to ignore those things and say, 'Oh, we're all just one humanity,' is another extreme that I think is unhelpful."

"Naïve?" I suggest.

"It is naïve. And it's more often said by people in a dominant position. Unlike people who have experienced this personally."

Judy Roitman

"My concern about the future is the tendency of people to try to use practice for self-improvement," Judy Roitman tells me. "It's all over the place! And it shows itself in all kinds of forms. You know, there was this great quote that someone posted on Facebook, a Tibetan guy – and Zen Master Seung Sahn used to say something like this too – he said, 'Our practice isn't about feeling comfortable.' Zen Master Seung Sahn said, 'You want peace? Go to the movies.' It's not about feeling comfortable. You're *supposed* to feel bad. He didn't say, 'feel bad.' It was a better phrase. But if you're not made uncomfortable by practice, you're not practicing. You have to question everything. You have to look at the hard stuff and question everything. And cut through it. Really. So I am concerned about people not being willing to do that, not understanding that that's really the essence of practice. It's not about feeling comfortable and feeling good, but it's about something that's much bigger than you are.

"So if I have a concern, that would be my concern, this cultural thing of people wanting self-aggrandizement and wanting to feel better all the time, and that's their yardstick."

Meido Moore

"I don't think the core of the tradition will go away," Meido Moore muses. "I suspect it will survive. But what I'm concerned about are things using the name Zen – making use of its marketing cachet– and misrepresenting themselves thereby. I'm concerned with the conflation of Western psychotherapy and Zen, for example. I'm concerned about the so-called secular Buddhist movement which in many cases is not Buddhist; there's no need to call it that."

"You're referring to the Mindfulness phenomenon?"

"Mindfulness itself, the practice itself is fine. But I think there are authors, some of whom have quite a lot of traction, who essentially espouse a physical-materialist view which is among the views specifically refuted by the Buddha. They discuss core Buddhist teachings like karma and rebirth as if they were just something that the Buddha decided to teach in order to accord with the views prevalent during his time, which is not true at all. The Buddha recast these teachings in some very interesting ways which ran counter to what was going on at that time.

"But in any case, there are people who do not go profoundly into the tradition, master the tradition, and then are quick to say, 'Oh, we need to change it; we need to transform it. We need to throw this out; we need to throw that out.' At some point, there are a lot of babies being thrown out with the bath water.

"There's a big chunk of stuff called Zen in the West which – to my mind – is no longer Zen and arguably not even Buddhist anymore, and yet still has the outer trappings of people shaving their heads, wearing robes, and so on. I have concern about that. It's a misrepresentation of the tradition; it's a watering down of the tradition, especially if you remove the core of the whole practice: awakening or kensho that is the linchpin of the teaching that Bodhidharma brought from China. Without this thing we call kensho, there's not much left that couldn't be provided in a better manner through something like psychotherapy or just a simple mindfulness practice. So what I'm complaining about is sloppy modernism, the deconstruction of the tradition in a way that – to me – seems rather haphazard, uninformed, and careless."

"The teacher with whom I studied for a long time – Albert Low – said, 'If you take awakening out of Buddhism, it doesn't have much to offer.'"[98]

---

98   Cf. *Zen Conversations*, p. 49: "Nowadays in the West the pure waters of Zen are being muddied, and more and more it is said that Buddha and the patriarchs did not really mean one should search for one's true nature. Some say the essence of the Way is living an ethical life, others advocate just sitting in meditation and forcing oneself to take up the lotus posture even at risk of knees and ankles. Others prefer to read books and attend conferences. But the word Buddha means awakened. To be awakened is to be awakened in, and therefore to, true nature.

"What else is it? What else was it that resolved Shakymuni's quest? Or Dogen's quest? Or Hakuin's spiritual quest? Yeah. I like Albert's writings by the way."

James Córdova

James Córdova tells me, "You know, the thing I worry about the most these days ... I don't know what to call it. The sort of gigification of ..."

"Sorry, the what?"

"Gigification. I'm making a word up. That Dharma teaching can be a person's gig. 'This is what I do.' And not from a place of calling or of service but more from a place of, 'This is how I make my living.' Or, 'This is where I get my sense of self-worth.' I am so allergic to that that I'm prone to Type 1 error to some degree. I think the disservice is in both directions. I think it has the potential of being overly narrowing of the teacher to disengage from the rest of the society and culture. And I think more perniciously is the way that it can, almost loftily, serve to inflate the ego. The teacher-and-student relationship is transactional, but if you're always in the teacher role and you're always receiving this genuflection, the head can become quite large."

Debra Seido Martin

"I am concerned with how our practice adapts to the needs of the times without losing its depth and roots," Debra Martin tells me. "I am concerned for the young, most of whom are very astute about social injustice and the ecological crisis they are inheriting. They're also diverse and psychologically astute. They don't want the iconoclastic go-it-alone Zen of the babyboomers but a practice that is grounded in reality and is collective in nature. I want to support how they face a troubled world careening towards a future I can only imagine. Particularly in my experience as a therapist and Zen teacher, I want to support *full* integration of the practice that embraces the healing of trauma alongside the truth of 'beyond self.'

"For the first time in human history, it's a distinct possibility we might not go on. The times yearn for a different collective consciousness than the one fueling the fragmentation of our society, widespread ecological collapse, and the war in Ukraine. We are heading rapidly into this unknown together, like it

---

Zen teachers who teach anything less than this are cheating their students ... Without awakening, kensho, satori, call it what you will, Buddhism has very little to offer the West except more abstruse philosophy and an ethical system in no way superior to the Christians." [from *The World: A Gateway*, Tuttle Publishing, 1995]

or not. The koan can't be answered by the individual, and yet we're each called to respond. It's important to me to address the moment in our place of practice rather than have Zen be a place to avoid the complexities of what is happening and what our role can be."

"Okay, so what does Zen have to offer the members of the generation my grandchildren belong to, who have to face these issues in a way I was privileged not to have had to face them? In this current situation, what does Zen potentially offer my grandchildren?"

"A way to be fully alive and awake and responsive to the incredible challenges we face. Not hide in despair or rage or numbness. That's true empowerment, to use a more conventional term."

Sarah Bender

"In order to continue," Sarah Bender reflects, "I think it really is essential for us to become more and more aware of the cultural legacies not only of Japan and China but also of this place where we live, our own blindnesses."

"Such as?"

"To recognize the ways in which we've been able to not notice that we're consuming something like thirty-six times more than someone living in India, and the actual allowable amount of carbon for a person. So looking at that.

"Something Robert Thurman[99] said once really stuck for me. When Buddhism first came to Tibet from India there was this effort to translate all of the writings that were coming from India into the Tibetan language. Americans, on the other hand, want to translate American writings into other languages. So there is that kind of arrogance in our culture. Right now, for example, a Tai Chi class is happening in my driveway led by the abbot of the Vietnamese temple in town. And one of the members was enthralled by what he was doing, his presence and the way he was teaching us, and invited him to give a talk someplace else. And when he went and gave the talk, she was kind of shocked. 'Wow! He has these very strict views about how you do things and about how you address the teacher and about not being reborn and about – you know – greed, hatred, and ignorance.' And I thought, 'Yeah. That's one reason why I invited him to come and teach here.' We need to listen to people whose traditions are embedded in other cultures, who are still practicing in those cultures, and we need to look at our own cultural arrogance."

---

99 Buddhist scholar. The first westerner to be ordained by the Dalai Lama in the Tibetan Gelug tradition.

Roger Brennan

Roger Brennan was invited to comment on a paper dealing with the issue of Buddhism and social justice. "And I have not been able to do it. I'm interested in Zen meditation. Buddhist philosophy, Buddhism as a religion is not where my real interest is, and I would have to say that I have a very little understanding of it. So a lot of stuff you hear in teishos and stuff, I just let it go. It's not where my interest is. I'm a Christian. But I would say that one of the reasons I can't write a commentary on that paper on Buddhism and social justice is because I don't see it. Because my experience has been that many people I know who are doing Zen are doing it for themselves, much as I am. And in all the years and all the groups I've been with, I've never seen a powerful thrust or need to be involved in issues of justice. So from my perspective as a Christian that's something, in my experience anyway, that Zen lacks. Zen talks compassion, but for me it's theoretical because I don't see it being brought into daily reality. Individual people may be involved in charitable activities. Sr. Elaine, for example, has set up an organization for bringing Zen and yoga to people in prisons. And we have the situation with refugees now; people might want to make a contribution to that. But I don't think the people I know would see getting involved in these as a demand of their Zen practice.

"When we say in the Four Great Aspirations that we desire to free all creatures, I feel that without an analysis of the causes of unfreedom, it's hard to take practical effective action to change things. And for me, as a Christian, that's essential. Perhaps that's something Christianity could bring to Zen, but, given the underlying teaching that 'everything is perfect just as it is,' I don't know how."

Chris Amirault

"I think Zen needs to develop some understanding of how to approach issues of identity and structural power and history that doesn't involve playing the 'no self' card," Chris Amirault tells me as we discuss the membership of Shining Window Zen. "In our sangha we have had someone with MS with very little physical control except a little bit of speech. We have had somebody who is transgender. There is a regular who identifies primarily as Potawatomi and another who is an African American woman with visual disabilities. We have somebody who identifies as queer and bisexual. For those folks, having a Zen teacher who feels comfortable about identity in the context of Zen practice is one of the appealing features of what the practice brings. If I had said to them, 'Look, here in Zen we don't talk about identity and self, because there is no such thing as a permanent self,' there would be like one person sitting with me. So

I've learned a lot from the Larry Yangs[100] and the Ruth Kings,[101] and the Insight folks about approaches to fit some of the Zen Buddhist Mahayana traditions around these questions in ways that I think honor the traditions but also don't dismiss people's genuine concerns. So that's one thing I think about a lot.

"The Boundless Way Zen collective is grappling with other questions as well. Climate change is an existential crisis because it's not actually about the world going up in flames, it's about human society going up in flames. As Native American traditions like to remind us, the Earth is going to be just fine. The Earth is really not concerned about the human project. And humans better think about how to perpetuate the human project on this Earth, 'cause this Earth is not going to continue to sustain it. And I think this will increasingly be a feature of why people come to Zen practice."

"How so?" I ask. "What concrete benefit does Zen have for helping people deal with these issues?"

"Speaking from my own meager insight derived from this practice, my relationship to the 10,000 things is fundamentally different than it used to be. And my care for those 10,000 things has shifted. At least in my perspective, I experience the world of my environment with a greater level of awareness and sensitivity. I would not have characterized myself as an environmentalist fifteen years ago but would now, and I don't think that's a political shift. It's a spiritual shift."

Kate Hartland

"As far as I can tell," Kate Hartland tells me, "Zen is the best system – and I use the word 'system' lightly; I mean, I just need a word to put in there – the best system for coming to a realization of who we really are. And if we don't know who we really are, we can really make a mess of things for ourselves and others. So here is this system tested over millennia that I think makes it worth preserving."

"It is also," I point out, "a system which has undergone a great deal of modification since it first arose in China."

"Yes! And this is part of what I love about Zen, that it's alive. My brother is a Baptist minister, and when I speak with him – and I don't want to speak ill of Christianity because I see how good it has been in his life – but there's something that's dead about it because it all goes back to this one book that was written a long time ago and nothing can be changed. But Zen is alive. It's

---

100 *Awakening Together: The Spiritual Practice of Inclusivity and Community.* Wisdom, 2017.

101 *Mindful of Race: Transforming Racism from the Inside.* Sounds True, 2018.

changed in every culture that it has met up with. The way that it's practiced changes, although the core always reflects the truth. And I see that happening here in this country as we try to find what is its relevance here, what models work. It's not a monastic model on the ascendance in this country. It is a lay model, at least among the practitioners if not the teachers. I don't know what will be the way it eventually works best here, but I think we're trying out many different ways, and there are lots of possibilities."

"What are the primary challenges at the moment? For Zen in 21st century North America."

"Well, first of all, awakening happens regardless of Zen. It's not dependent upon this practice. So, should the entire practice of Zen die away, someone will reinvent it according to their culture. So there's nothing that can get lost. Reality is this way. And if we just look, we will find this way out.

"One challenge is whether or not to be actively aligned with social justice causes. Personally, I veer away from this approach, preferring to let the teaching and practice develop the person to be more effective in whatever cause she chooses to take up. I think another big challenge is that there is no central governing organization. That's both a strength and a weakness. It seems like we are trying to find more governance but still wanting to maintain independence in teaching. But how do you do that? One experiment is the 'asanga' model used by the White Plum Asanga.[102] They have created a self-governing consortium of teachers who independently lead their individual groups. They call it an 'affinity organization of peers.'

"Some of us are struggling to find some other model than those we have experienced that supports teachers so that we can teach and be useful and relevant. Somehow teachers were supposed to be a finished product. That just is not my experience nor that of several others. We feel that we need to be responsible or accountable to one another; that we need to continue within our practice to have time to do that. When you're running retreats there's very little time to just sit quietly. And I've felt the great lack of that and have tried to put it back into the retreats that we have now. And I feel we are just constantly having to reinvent what works for us. There's nothing to fall back on."

Lila Dené Redding

The 1960s – when Rafe Martin and John Pulleyn first came to the Rochester Zen Center – were a politically volatile time. Philip Kapleau, however, actively discouraged students from becoming involved in political issues. Their

---

[102] Established by Taizan Maezumi and made up of his immediate heirs and their successors.

focus, he insisted, should be on zazen and the effort to achieve awakening. But as Scott Thornton – quoting Bob Dylan – said, "The times, they are a-changin'."

Lila Redding is the Sangha Programs Coordinator at the Rochester Zen Center. "One of the things that happened with the pandemic and all of the riots following the police killing of George Floyd[103] is that Zen Center started reflecting on our place in this, our responsibility in this. What can we contribute in a good way to racial justice at large? So we ended up developing a group that organizes different programming around racial justice issues. When there was a lot of anti-Asian violence happening this past spring, we had a conversation on that with a woman who is an Asian-American Buddhist practitioner, just trying to understand her experience with being Asian and practicing in a mostly white sangha.

"So my role, what happens is somebody comes and says, 'I want to host this program, how do I make it happen?' So it's taking sangha members' ideas and trying to bring them to life. We have more ideas than we can put on the ground and run with right now, so we really have to prioritize what projects we have space for."

"The community takes the initiative in identifying the issues that they want to find some way of incorporating into their practice?" I ask.

"I think just being able to deal with collectively. It's so easy for people to come to the zendo and sit and then go home. But we want to be able to get to know each other. So there's a kind of community development sort of aspect to this too, and these collaborative kinds of social engagement projects give us something to come together on. Also social justice is generally an interest in our sangha. People want to learn more about their own personal biases, be able to figure out how to come together collectively on some of these issues."

The first concern she focused on in her position was anti-trans bias.

"We have a sangha member who identifies as non-binary, and they came out as being non-binary while a member of the Zen Center. And they were struggling with the fact that people were having a hard time using 'they/them' pronouns and identifying them correctly. And they are also somebody who's a fantastic organizer; they had experience doing event coordination. And I wanted to get their help in doing some other programming that we were doing, but I also wanted to support them in living in a community that could *appropriately* support them. And so I threw out the idea why don't we do some programming around anti-trans bias so that they can find support in an organization that knows how to support them.

---

103 George Floyd was an African-American killed by police officers in Minneapolis, Minnesota, on May 25, 2020.

"So when we did this 'Anti-Trans Bias in the Media,' we didn't really know what skills we had to bring to the table. We didn't really know if we knew how to make it go. And so we kept programming mostly in-house, but some of the trans-people at the Zen Center ended up inviting their friends over. So their first exposure to the Zen Center was through this anti-trans bias conversation. And since then we've realized that every time we host a program like this, we have to find out who in the community would have some interest in this topic. So we are very intentionally reaching out to different members of the Rochester community. And then we're starting to think about how can we bridge these gaps for people in a bigger way?

"I think this is something that Buddhist groups are struggling with in general right now. If you think about it, I think there's no point in our history where we've been as diverse as we are now. Monasteries were usually all men of the same nationality and race, and we don't have that anymore. We have a whole range of genders; we have a whole range of sexuality; we have a whole range of races that are trying to figure how to come together and make this thing work for all of us. And at the same time, there is this immense wealth of knowledge that a trans person – say – can bring to the Dharma on gender that hadn't really had a place so prominently before when it was more a monolithic group that was coming together. So I think as we become more diverse, we learn more about what resources we each bring to the table depending on where we're coming from that adds to the Dharma in general. It can be the stuff that divides us, but it can also be the stuff that brings us together."

Donna Kowal

"One of the conversations we've been having is how the Zen Center can be more of a resource to the community that we live in," Donna Kowal adds. "If we're going to do that, we have to recognize the barriers that exist. For instance, our center can look pretty intimidating on the outside, particularly if you're not college educated, middle class, and white. So, to adapt to a community that is increasingly more diverse, we have to rethink not the teaching but how we make it available to others. For example, during a brainstorming session we recently discussed the idea of offering introductory workshops in community spaces located in the neighborhoods where people live in addition to here at the Zen Center."

"This is something you're doing?"

"It's an idea we're exploring, along with many others for making the Center more accessible. It's part of ongoing conversations that have taken place, especially during the pandemic pause, which really offered us an opportunity to step back and look at ways we can be more responsive to the differing needs of people. For example, we recently added an all-gender changing room. Another is teaching how to sit in a way that is inclusive to all abilities. In the center's early years, Roshi Kapleau would have emphasized full-lotus as the ideal to strive for. Based on the rigors of the Zen tradition, you might even get the impression that you need to have a certain body in order to practice. More and more, we're teaching people how to sit in a chair and use a meditation bench effectively, covering them equally with how to sit in a cross-legged position. And we never say that one way is absolutely better than the other. What matters most is that you sit still."

"So as a community you're reflecting on ways in which you may not have been inclusive in the past or perhaps not as flexible in the past and, in looking at these, seeking ways to adapt your presentation accordingly. Is that it?"

"Yes."

"So one of the things that several of Roshi Kapleau's direct heirs have spoken to me about is that, during their time of training, there had been more emphasis placed on the attainment of prajna/wisdom than on karuna/compassion. Do you see any change in that?"

"The two have always been there, but the wisdom part – prajna – was more overt, more on the front burner. Another initiative that happened during the pandemic was the creation of a Sangha Programs Office. It's run by staff and volunteers, and it's all about community engagement. Zen Center events and activities outside the context of sittings help people to get to know one another and feel socially connected, so they're a good vessel to promote the more compassionate dimension of practice. But while the two have always been there, until recently they haven't always been expressed equally."

"Why not? Why did it take so long for there to be that balance in North American Zen?"

"I don't think it was intentional; I think it was just a matter of tradition. Having a tradition is important. Traditions can ground us and help us see that we're part of something bigger, a lineage let's say. But at the same time, when we cling to tradition, or cling to doing things the way we've always done them, we're not seeing things as they are right now. We're not adapting to change. Just in the past two decades, there's been incredible changes due to globalization, climate change, human migration, and technology."

Epilogue
ONLINE

The first interest – slight as it was – shown to Buddhism in the West came about during the late 19th and early 20th centuries, when belief in Christian doctrine was being challenged by the biological and geological sciences as well as anthropological research. The interest came in two forms. Some were intrigued by the fact that the worldview of Buddhism was more in line with the findings of the scientific community than biblically-based systems of thought appeared to be. For others, the interest came from the allure of the exotic. In popular literature and the press, Buddhism was often linked with spiritualism and various forms of psychic phenomenon such as the claim of the founder of the Theosophical movement, Helena Blavatsky, that she received spiritual instruction telepathically from secret masters residing in the Himalayas. When interest in Zen arose some decades later, it was seen as a more rational form of Buddhism than what the Theosophists and others promoted, and yet it, too, retained the appeal of the exotic. As Zen continues to be modified by the West, it will inevitably become more mundane. That's a good thing although there will always be people who regret the loss of the old ambiance.

As I've noted elsewhere, Zen has become close to mainstream in the west. The word itself has been anglicized to suggest the ability to remain unshaken by events over which one has no control, a sophisticated appreciation of natural aesthetics, and what Sarah Bender called the "radical simplicity" of style, all with overtones of spiritual wisdom. Still for a long while, many found the idea of visiting a physical Zen Center or temple – much less a Zen monastery – daunting. Then suddenly they were available for all to visit online.

The COVID-19 pandemic shut down schools, universities, health clubs, entertainment facilities, restaurants, and religious gatherings. Video conferencing became the only option for many of these institutions – including Zen Centers – and the stock value of the video conferencing service Zoom increased by 450 percent in a single year. Surprisingly, what began as a necessity for Zen communities proved, in many places, to be a positive benefit.

David Weinstein

"The Rockridge Meditation Community doesn't physically exist any longer," David Weinstein tells me. "With the pandemic, we couldn't keep paying rent on a building we couldn't use. We've gotten together physically a handful of times, but there's no plan to be at another physical building at this point."

"What is the plan then?"

"Well, if it's not broke, don't fix it. Zoom seems to be working just fine. Actually better because now on a Wednesday evening when we get together, there are people from the East Coast, Arizona, Colorado, Washington State, Montreal, Oaxaca, Bali, all over the place who participate regularly, and that didn't happen when we had a physical place. The participation is greater and richer for that."

"What's the format like?"

"We gather at 7:00, and either I or someone I've invited to host the gathering will present a koan. We'll sit for a period of meditation. The person who is hosting will say something about their experience with the koan and then open it up for others to share. I tend to break everybody up into breakout groups so people get a chance to talk with each other in a smaller, more intimate environment. Rather than 20 or 30 people listening to a handful of people say something because of time limitations, they have 20 minutes in a three- or four-person group. Which is something I was doing when we were meeting physically also. I used to send people off to different parts of the building to have a conversation. Then we come back together again, and there's usually 15 or 20 minutes left to share with one another in the larger group. That's an important part of the practice. Harada Roshi, the founder of the tradition that is part of our tradition, said that without that kind of conversation, 'There is no Zen'. Then we end with a recording of the Vows."

"A recording of the Vows?"

"Well, you can't really all chant together because of the way Zoom works. If I were musically inclined or had a better voice, or someone else did, they'd be welcome to perform the vows as everybody else listened. As it is with their microphones muted, folks do get into singing and sometimes gesticulating as they sing ..." He shrugs. "Anyway, we've had eight online retreats since the pandemic restrictions were put in place."

"And how did that work?"

"Well, a lot easier than an in-person retreat. You don't have to carry cushions, and you don't have to negotiate with people who snore and changing room assignments. Wonderful for the integration of the practice into life. We're practicing in our homes. Right? There's not the question of after the retreat is over and I go home, how do I bring the retreat home with me? We invite people to explore that as we are in retreat, the boundary between home and retreat."

"It sounds as if it's a format you're fond of."

"We're going to have our first in-person retreat in June [2022], and the leadership – the teachers and some of the leadership of PZI – have had two or three in-person retreats during the pandemic. Being in-person is definitely different than being on Zoom or Skype or whatever, and there are a lot of advantages to that, benefits, no doubt. But right at this point, yes, I think we're all fond of the way the Zoom retreats are inclusive. We have people in Kenya, Sri Lanka, Amsterdam, Scotland, and Canada, who are in all different times zones. We have two starting times, an East Coast starting time and a West Coast starting time. There are East Coast ending times and West Coast ending times as well. We have conversations with students, as we would, except they're all scheduled, and they're all on Zoom. It's just very easy.

"Occasionally, a member of the Rockridge community will send me a message asking, 'When are we going to start looking for a place to sit together?' My response has been, 'As soon as you start looking. I'm quite happy with it the way things are right now.' I'm open to other possibilities, but I do not have the energy to go out and find a place, and the Pacific Zen Institute does not have the resources to pay for one now either. So, if we find a place, that's great, but we are going to have to pay for it ourselves. And that stops the conversation."

Chris Amirault

"At Shining Window Zen, we hold our sesshins on Zoom and have largely been online since things shut down in 2020," Chris Amirault informs me. "A bunch of us have done quite a few of them and have a pretty good sense of the rhythm of it. And there's some very interesting advantages in integrating sesshin into home practice and samu and things like that."

"How do you integrate samu into distance practice?" I ask. "Go wash the dishes?"

"Yeah. Exactly. It's work practice around caretaking of your environment, I think is the language we use. So whether it's outdoor gardening or doing the dishes, whatever. Integrating practice off the cushion has never been a challenge for me, but I think for a lot of people it's a different approach.

"So the way the online Boundless Way sesshins have been structured ..." He counts on his fingers as he reviews the format in his mind. "I guess five two-hour or two-and-half-hour chunks separated by two hours."

"So you log on for these ..."

"Right. So I log on at 6:00, I think it starts at 7:00 on the East Coast, 6:00 here locally in Tulsa. And then it's mostly the same. There's no *oryoki*.[104] I think that's the only major omission, but the encouragement is to approach meals in that spirit."

I ask how they do dokusan.

"I actually think this is great. If you show up for sesshin, you're in dokusan. You don't get to pass. They just kick you in."

"You mean you're sitting there and suddenly the screen just lights up?"

"Yeah, and all of sudden there's Bob Waldinger[105] or somebody."

"With no warning."

"No, no warning."

"So you're seated, focusing your attention, and suddenly there's a teacher staring at you."

"Exactly. Yeah. I love it."

Lila Dené Redding

I ask Lila Redding how COVID impacted the Rochester community.

"I think we're still figuring that out, really. New York State was the first state to lockdown, and, even before that lockdown happened, we had a sangha member who said, 'Hey, I think you really need to get on Zoom. I will pay you to get on Zoom.' So they offered a donation to start our first account, and we got our sitting schedule set up on Zoom. It's not the same as the daily sitting schedule that staff do, but when that started we were suddenly getting sixty-plus people to the sittings every morning."

"And that's more than you would have expected before the pandemic?"

"If we were meeting in person – if you counted staff too – we would maybe have twenty. But we have sangha members nationwide and internationally, and they're now able to participate in the sittings too. Our numbers are down a little bit since people were able to sit in-person again, but we're still looking at fifty people for our morning sittings. And whenever we do programming, we're able to include people who don't live in Rochester."

"Does that mean you're going to look at ways to continue to accommodate those distance-members in the future?"

"That's the intention. Absolutely. All of our sesshins now are hybrid so that people can participate from home. And we're going to continue doing daily

---

104 A stylized monastic way of eating using three nested bowls and chopsticks.

105 Cf. *Zen Conversations*, Pp. 9; 21; 43-44; 58; 87.

sittings. We're going to continue doing programming that is on Zoom. That is not going away."

"How does a hybrid-sesshin work?"

"So there are, like, forty people who go to sesshin in-person. We still have a lot of COVID protocol that goes along with that. Everybody's vaccinated, everybody comes with a negative PCR test that's been in the last 72 hours. We're still wearing masks whenever we're moving about the building. It's all running like normal sesshin schedule. Minus the chanting and the formal meals. We haven't brought those back yet."

"Why did you drop the chanting?"

"Because there's science that says whenever you project your voice, the virus spreads faster. And then at the same time that that's happening, there are monitors who are operating at computers instead of in the zendo who are making sure that the tech end of things is going well. The people who are on Zoom can still hear all the bells and clappers that are happening in the zendo. So they're following the same schedule that we follow during sesshin."

Dosho Port

Dosho Port and Tetsugan Zummach have been engaged in online Zen since 2013, well before the pandemic.

"We tried a few times to start a center that would be something like a Zen Center in the early model," Dosho explains. "But I think in terms of intensity of practice, the horse already had left the barn in terms of what was culturally possible by that time. We didn't find enough people in the locations we were in to generate the kind of energy that's necessary. And people that came were not interested in doing that kind of training by and large. There were a few here and a few there that are still with us. But mostly – you know – these are really tough times. People are having a hell of a hard time and looking for a little peace. 'Can you teach me just how to enjoy this breath?' And sure we can. That's great. And, of course, it's a benefit for people that we can offer that. But that is not the extent of what's available in the Buddhadharma. So gradually we started doing this work online. We didn't really plan it in that way, but what's happened is that our online group has actually become the training group that we were trying to start through in-person centers."

Their online group is the Vine of Obstacles: Online Support for Zen Training. The homepage of the site states that the program is "designed for practitioners living at home who yearn to realize the great matter of birth and death."

"With the technology we have now, it's possible with online work and in-person sesshin – which I continue to think is really important – to practice with vigor. So we have daily zazen for people, retreats, Dharma talks, and practice meetings. Most importantly, we have practice commitments. We have practice check-ins, so there's an accountability system, there's an integrity system. People not only say they're practicing but they follow through. If they don't, it's visible and it's an issue to talk about. And of course, as householders it's different than when somebody's living in residential or monastic practice. For example, there are things you have to do if your ten-year-old is sick. We understand that. And yet it's possible for householders, instead of the usual thing of fitting in practice around your life, to fit in your life around your practice. To make your practice your main thing. That's the difference."

The practice commitment includes a minimum of five hours of zazen a week –"some do closer to fifteen" – weekly Dharma talks, weekly individual meetings with either Dosho or Tetsugan, and group study using a text-based program, "an online platform like all the universities now use for study and interaction.

"It's possible with this format to go much more deeply especially in the study aspect than the Zen Center model allows. I've taught for years in Zen Centers, and mostly what happens is people come once a week. You might give a reading assignment. They come the next week or not, have done the reading or not. You have a little time to work on something, and they go home. Through the text-based online program, there is a continuity of daily practice for people living anywhere on the planet.

"And people get to know each other because they share the details of their life and practice as a part of studying together. They share stuff about their practice that is much more personal than what people at in-person Zen Centers would ever hear about from each other. I've practiced as a student and as a teacher at in-person Zen Centers where you come in, sit facing the wall, maybe say 'hi,' and maybe chat for a moment on the way to the car. Or in sesshin, of course, you're just sitting there and nobody's talking. So you really don't know much about anyone else's life let alone their Dharma process. Here with our Vine practice everyone knows a lot about each other's processes. Sometimes it becomes an issue to set limits on what is shared, especially in terms of koan work, because that, of course, needs to be private. But there is great learning this way, perhaps akin to the difference between individual and group therapy. So a strong sense of sangha develops."

Zen, as Dosho points out, involves a heart-to-heart relationship between student and teacher. Where a student happens to live is less important than their affinity with a teacher.

•••

There is a saying sometimes erroneously attributed to the Buddha which states that when the student is ready, the teacher will appear. It actually comes from Blavatsky's Theosophical movement with its claims about the possibility of telepathic instruction from distant teachers. Remarkably, with the technology now available and a few keystrokes, when the student is ready, the teacher actually can appear.

As Karin Kempe notes, the forms in which Zen will be presented in the future are unknowable. Maybe the robes and Asian accoutrements will remain. Maybe zendos – if they are called that – will be furnished with chairs instead of cushions and mats. Maybe chants will continue to be in Pali or Japanese. Maybe they will be scored for Gregorian chant, something James Ford tells me Jiyu Kennett actually did. These are all fairly superficial matters.

The important thing, as Kate Hartland point outs, is that the central insight of Zen – awakening – is not unique to it, and, because awakening is universal, it will continue to be experienced and shared. The new forms of instruction that arise may well still be called Zen, and the trappings may be as stable and persistent as Vatican protocols. Or they may be as different from what we are familiar with today as online instruction is from the Asian temples where the pioneers who brought the practice to the West studied. As Hogen Bays notes, the most fundamental of all Buddhist teachings is impermanence, the inevitability of change. That is one of the few things about which we can be absolutely certain.

Appendices

Appendix 1
THE PRECEPTS

As iterated by Great Vow Monastery in Oregon

The Three Pure Precepts
I vow not to commit evil.
I vow to cultivate goodness.
I vow to help others.

The Three Refuges
I take refuge in the Buddha.
I take refuge in the Dharma.
I take refuge in the Sangha.

The Ten Grave Precepts
I vow not to kill, but to cherish all life.
I vow not to steal, but to respect that which belongs to others.
I vow not to misuse sexual energy, but to be honest and respectful.
I vow not to lie, but to speak the truth.
I vow not to misuse drugs or alcohol, but to keep the mind clear.
I vow not to gossip about others' faults, but to be understanding and sympathetic.
I vow not to praise myself by criticizing others, but to overcome my own shortcomings.
I vow not to withhold spiritual or material aid, but to give freely when needed.
I vow not to unleash anger, but to seek its source.
I vow not to speak ill of the Three Treasures, but to cherish and uphold them.

As iterated by the Buddhist Temple of Ohio

The Three Treasures
Oneness, the Awakened nature of all beings. *I take refuge in the Buddha.*
Diversity, the ocean of wisdom and compassion. *I take refuge in the Dharma.*
Harmony, the interdependence of all. *I take refuge in the Sangha.*

The Three Pure Precepts
Not knowing, thereby giving up fixed ideas about myself and universe, *I vow to cease from evil.*
Bearing witness to the joy and suffering of the world, *I vow to practice good.*
Healing myself and others, *I vow to save all beings.*

The Ten Grave Precepts
Recognizing I am not separate from all that is, *I vow to take up the Way of Not Killing.*
Being satisfied with what I have, *I vow to take up the Way of Not Stealing.*
Treating all beings with respect and dignity, *I vow to take up the Way of Not Misusing Sexuality.*
Listening and speaking from the heart, *I vow to take up the Way of Not Speaking falsely.*
Cultivating a mind that sees clearly, *I vow to take up the Way of Not Intoxicating Mind and Body.*
Unconditionally accepting what each moment has to offer, *I vow to take up the Way of Not Discussing the Faults of Others.*
Speaking what I perceive to be the truth without guilt or blame, *I vow to take up the Way of Not Praising Myself While Abusing Others.*
Using all the ingredients of my life and Being Generous with the Fruits of my Dharma Practice, *I vow to take up the way of Not Sparing the Dharma Assets.*
Transforming suffering into wisdom, *I vow to take up the Way of Not Indulging in Anger.*
Honoring my life as an instrument of the Great Way, *I vow to take the Way of not Defaming the Three Treasures.*

As iterated by the Rochester Zen Center

The Three Treasures
I take refuge in Buddha,
    and resolve that with all beings
      I will understand the Great Way
      whereby the Buddha seed may forever thrive.
I take refuge in Dharma,
    and resolve that with all beings
      I will enter deeply into the sutra-treasure
      whereby my wisdom may grow as vast as the ocean.
I take refuge in Sangha,
    and in its wisdom, example, and never-failing help,
    and resolve to live in harmony with all sentient beings.

The Three General Resolutions
I resolve to avoid evil.
I resolve to do good.
I resolve to liberate all sentient beings.

The Ten Cardinal Precepts
I resolve not to kill,
    but to cherish all life.
I resolve not to take what is not given,
    but to respect the things of others.
I resolve not to misuse sexuality,
    but to be caring and responsible.
I resolve not to lie,
    but to speak the truth.
I resolve not to cause others to abuse alcohol or drugs,
    nor to do so myself, but to keep the mind clear.
I resolve not to speak of the faults of others,
    but to be understanding and sympathetic.
I resolve not to praise myself and disparage others,
    but to overcome my own shortcomings.
I resolve not to withhold spiritual or material aid,
    but to give them freely where needed.
I resolve not to indulge in anger,
    but to practice forbearance.
I resolve not to revile the Three Treasures,
    but to cherish and uphold them.

As iterated by the Kwan Um School

The Five
I vow to abstain from taking life.
I vow to abstain from taking things not given.
I vow to abstain from misconduct done in lust.
I vow to abstain from lying.
I vow to abstain from intoxicants taken to induce heedlessness.

The Ten
I vow to abstain from taking life.
I vow to abstain from taking things not given.
I vow to abstain from misconduct done in lust.
I vow to abstain from lying.
I vow to abstain from intoxicants taken to induce heedlessness.
I vow not to talk about the faults of others.
I vow not to praise myself and put down others.
I vow not to be covetous and to be generous.
I vow not to give way to anger and to be harmonious.
I vow not to slander the three jewels (Buddha, Dharma, Sangha)

The Sixteen
I vow to abstain from taking life.
I vow to abstain from taking things not given.
I vow to abstain from misconduct done in lust.
I vow to abstain from lying.
I vow to abstain from intoxicants taken to induce heedlessness.
I vow not to talk about the faults of others.
I vow not to praise myself and put down others.
I vow not to be covetous and to be generous.
I vow not to give way to anger and to be harmonious.
I vow not to slander the three jewels (Buddha, Dharma, Sangha).
I vow homage to the Buddha.
I vow homage to the Dharma.
I vow homage to the Sangha.
I vow generosity to people.
I vow compassionate speech and compassionate action toward people.
I vow together action with people and to become one and to attain the Buddha Way.

The Forty-Eight
To respect your teachers and friends.
Not to drink liquor.
Not to eat meat.
Not to eat the five pungent roots.
To always encourage one who has committed an offense to repent and reform.
To request the Dharma from teachers and make offerings to them.
To always go to places where Dharma is taught.
To not disavow the Mahayana.
To care well for the sick.
Not to possess implements for killing.
Not to act as an emissary to create hostility between warring parties.
Not to conduct business with evil intentions.
Not to speak badly of others.
Not to set fires that will harm wildlife.
Not to teach other doctrines (besides Mahayana).
To teach correctly, without desiring personal gain.
Not to use your Dharma position to extract favors from people of power.
Not to become a teacher if you do not have a clear understanding of the Buddha-Dharma.
Not to gossip or spread rumors or slander to create discord in the Sangha.
To always cultivate the practice of liberating sentient beings and encourage others to do likewise.
To be compassionate and not seek revenge.
To let go of all arrogance and request the teaching.
To let go of all resentment and arrogance and teach appropriately.
Not to desert the Three Jewels, and to always cultivate the Bodhisattva Path.
To skillfully administer all the resources of the Three Jewels with a compassionate mind.
Not to accept benefit for yourself alone.
Not to accept special invitations which single you out for deference while excluding other members of the practicing community.
Not to issue special invitations to monks.
Not to make a living through illicit or harmful means.
To handle temple affairs with integrity and not be duplicitous towards the teaching.
To always find ways to protect and rescue all persons and valuables of the Sangha.

Do not act in ways that would harm any being.
Do not watch or participate in improper activities.
To always keep to the Mahayana path.
To always keep the great vows of the Mahayana.
To always follow the precepts.
When doing retreats, to always avoid hazardous situations.
To always keep the correct seating order.
To cultivate merits and wisdom.
To not discriminate in giving the Bodhisattva Precepts.
To not become a teacher for personal gain.
To not use the precepts for harassment.
To not think of breaking the precepts.
To always honor and keep the precepts.
To always teach all beings.
To always take a respectful seat when teaching the Dharma.
Not to establish incorrect rules to control the Sangha.
Not to act in ways that destroy the Buddhadharma.

Appendix 2
The Bodhisattva Vows

The Montreal Zen Center

In English[106]
All beings, without number,
I vow to liberate.
Endless blind passions,
I vow to uproot.
Dharma gates, beyond measure,
I vow to penetrate.
The Great Way of Buddha,
I vow to attain.

In French
Tous les êtres innombrables,
    je fais voeu de libérer.
Les passions aveugles et sans fin,
    je fais voeu de vaincre.
Les barrières infinies du Dharma,
    je fais voeu de franchir.
La grande Voie du Bouddha,
    je fais voeu de l'atteindre.

Boundless Way Zen

Beings are numberless; I vow to free them.
Delusions are inexhaustible; I vow to end them.
Dharma gates are boundless; I vow to enter them.
The Buddha Way is unsurpassable; I vow to embody it.

---

106 Same as the Rochester Zen Center.

Sanbo Zen

Sentient beings are numberless
I vow to free them
Delusions are inexhaustible
I vow to end them
The Dharma gates are boundless
I vow to enter them
The Buddha's Way is unsurpassable
I vow to embody it — fully.

Pacific Zen Institute

I vow to wake all the beings of the world,
I vow to set endless heartache to rest,
I vow to walk through every wisdom gate,
I vow to live the great Buddha way.

Chobo-ji, Seattle
(Japanese and English)

SHU JO MU HEN SEI GAN DO,
However innumerable all beings are, we vow to care for them all.

BO NO MU JIN SEI GAN DAN,
However inexhaustible delusions are, we vow to relinquish them all.

HO MON MU RYO SEI GAN GAKU,
However immeasurable gates to truth are, we vow to enter them all.

BUTSU DO MU JO SEI GAN JO.
However endless the Buddha's way is, we vow to follow it.

San Francisco Zen Center

Beings are numberless, I vow to save them.
Delusions are inexhaustible, I vow to end them.
Dharma gates are boundless, I vow to enter them.
Buddha's Way is unsurpassable, I vow to become it.

Appendix 3
AFFIRMING FAITH IN MIND
(Xin Xin Ming)[107]

The Great Way is not difficult
for those who do not pick and choose.

When preferences are cast aside,
the Way stands clear and undisguised.

But even slight distinctions made
set earth and heaven far apart.

If you would clearly see the truth,
discard opinions pro and con.

To founder in dislike and like
is nothing but the mind's disease.

And not to see the Way's deep truth
disturbs the mind's essential peace.

The Way is perfect like vast space,
where there's no lack and no excess.

Our choice to choose and to reject
prevents our seeing this simple truth.

Both striving for the outer world as well as for the inner void
condemn us to entangled lives.

Just calmly see that all is One,
and by themselves false views will go.

---

107 From the Rochester Zen Center, *Chants and Recitations*.

Attempts to stop activity
will fill you with activity.

Remaining in duality,
you'll never know of unity.

And not to know this unity
lets conflict lead you far astray.

When you assert that things are real,
you miss their true reality.

But to assert that things are void
also misses reality.

The more you talk and think on this
the further from the truth you'll be.

Cut off all useless thoughts and words,
and there's nowhere you cannot go.

Returning to the root itself,
you'll find the meaning of all things.

If you pursue appearances,
you overlook the primal source.

Awakening is to go beyond
both emptiness as well as form.

All changes in this empty world
seem real because of ignorance.

Do not go searching for the truth,
just let those fond opinions go.

Abide not in duality;
refrain from all pursuit of it.

If there's a trace of right and wrong,
True-mind is lost, confused, distraught.

From One-mind comes duality,
but cling not even to this One.

When this One-mind rests undisturbed,
then nothing in the world offends.

And when no thing can give offense,
then all obstructions cease to be.

If all thought-objects disappear,
the thinking subject drops away.

For things are things because of mind,
as mind is mind because of things.

These two are merely relative,
and both at source are Emptiness.

In Emptiness these are not two,
yet in each are contained all forms.

Once coarse and fine are seen no more,
then how can there be taking sides?

The Great Way is without limit,
beyond the easy and the hard.

But those who hold to narrow views are fearful and irresolute;
their frantic haste just slows them down.

If you're attached to anything,
you surely will go far astray.

Just let go now of clinging mind, and all things are just as they are:
In essence nothing goes or stays.

See into the true self of things, and you're in step with the Great Way,
thus walking freely, undisturbed.

But live in bondage to your thoughts,
and you will be confused, unclear.

This heavy burden weighs you down—
so why keep judging good and bad ?

If you would walk the highest Way,
do not reject the sense domain.

For as it is, whole and complete,
this sense world is Enlightenment.

The wise do not strive after goals;
the foolish put themselves in bonds.

The One Way knows no differences;
the foolish cling to this and that.

To seek Great Mind with thinking mind
is certainly a grave mistake.

From small mind come rest and unrest,
but mind awakened transcends both.

Delusion spawns dualities—these dreams are merely flowers of air—
why work so hard at grasping them?

Both gain and loss, and right and wrong—
once and for all get rid of them.

When you no longer are asleep,
all dreams will vanish by themselves.

If mind does not discriminate, all things are as they are, as One.
To go to this mysterious Source frees us from all entanglements.

When all is seen with 'equal mind,'
to our Self-nature we return.

This single mind goes right beyond
all reasons and comparison.

Make movement rest, and nothing moves;
see rest in motion—there's no rest.

When rest and movement cease to be,
then even oneness disappears.

This ultimate finality,
beyond all laws, can't be described.

With single mind one with the Way, all ego-centered strivings cease;
Doubts and confusion disappear, and so true faith pervades our life.

There is no thing that clings to us,
and nothing that is left behind.

All's self-revealing, void and clear,
without exerting power of mind.

Thought cannot reach this state of truth,
here feelings are of no avail.

In this true world of Emptiness,
both self and other are no more.

To enter this true empty world,
immediately affirm 'not-two.'

In this 'not-two' all is the same, with nothing separate or outside.
The wise in all times and places awaken to this primal truth.

The Way's beyond all space, all time;
one instant is ten thousand years.

Not only here, not only there,
truth's right before your very eyes.

Distinctions such as large and small
have relevance for you no more.

The largest is the smallest too—
here limitations have no place.

What is is not, what is not is—
if this is not yet clear to you, you're still far from the inner truth.

One thing is all, all things are one—
know this and all's whole and complete.

When faith and Mind are not separate, and not separate are Mind and faith,
this is beyond all words, all thought.

For here there is no yesterday,
no tomorrow,
no today.

Appendix 4
Torei Enji's Bodhisattva's Vow

When I regard the true nature of all things and all living creatures,
 I find them to be the sacred forms of the Tathagatha's never-failing essence.

Each particle of matter, each moment, is no other than the Tathagatha's inexpressible radiance.

With this realisation, our noble ancestors gave tender care to beasts and birds, with compassionate minds and hearts.

Among us, in our own daily lives, who is not reverently grateful for the protections of life: food, drink and clothing!
Though they are inanimate things, that are nonetheless the warm flesh and blood, the merciful incarnations of Buddha.

All the more, we can be especially understanding and affectionate with foolish people,
particularly with someone who becomes a sworn enemy and persecutes us with abusive language.
That very abuse conveys the Buddha's boundless loving-kindness.
It is a compassionate device to liberate us entirely from the mean spirited delusions we have built up with our wrongful conduct from the beginningless past.

With our open response to such abuse we completely relinquish ourselves, and the most profound and pure faith arises.
At the peak of each thought a lotus flower opens, and on each flower there is revealed a Buddha.
Everywhere is the Pure Land in its beauty.
We see fully the Tathagata's radiant light right where we are.

May we retain this mind and extend it throughout the world
 so that we and all beings become mature in Buddha's wisdom.

The Interviews

Index

Abbot, Hadrian – April 20, 2013; Sept 7, 2014; March 3, 2022. Pp. 124-25.
Amirault, Chris – Sept 9, 2021; Dec 9, 2021. Pp. 99-100; 145-46; 153-54.
Bays, Hogen – Oct 21, 2021; Nov 23, 2021. Pp. 47-48; 63-65; 119; 133-34; 157.
Bender, Sarah – Oct 30, 2013; July 19, 2022. Pp. 51-52; 59; 113-14; 144; 151.
Brennan, Roger – Aug 6, 2015; Sept 10, 2015; May 25, 2016. Pp. 39-42; 94-95; 145.
Byrnes, Joshin – May 30, 2022; Aug 2, 2022. Pp. 68-69; 137-39.
Carlson, Gyokuko – May 17, 2022. Pp. 102-03.
Cooper, Seiso Paul – March 24, 2020; May 20, 2020; July 28, 2022. Pp. 43-44; 61-62; 75; 81-85; 118.
Córdova, James – April 27, 2022. Pp. 67-68; 75; 80-81; 99; 122-23; 143.
Dempsey, Erin Joen – Oct 2, 2021; Jan 22, 2022. Pp. 85-87; 119.
Foisy, Jean-Luc – Nov 2, 2021; Jan 13, 2022. Pp. 101-02; 131-33.
Ford, James – May 4, 2013; May 14, 2018; May 12, 2022. Pp. 55-57; 92; 157.
Forstman, Valerie – Sept 8, 2018; March 21, 2022; May 10, 2022. Pp. 29; 66-67.
Haederle, Zenshin Michael – Jan 29, 2014; Sept 22, 2020. Pp. 95-98.
Hartland, Kate – Aug 18, 2022. Pp. 46; 146-47; 157.
Henkel, Kokyo – April 9, 2020; Dec 21, 2021. Pp. 20-23; 73-74; 123.
Kear, Cynthia – March 31, 2022; July 21, 2022. Pp. 17-20; 50; 100-01; 134-40.
Kempe, Karin – June 28, 2022. Pp. 44-45; 69-70; 98-99; 113; 131; 157.
Kowal, Donna – Oct 28, 2021; Dec 8, 2021. Pp. 121-22; 149-50.
Leizerman, Michael – Oct 5, 2021; Nov 30, 2021. Pp. 103-04; 119-21.
Martin, Debra Seido – March 18, 2022. Pp. 87-88; 91; 117-18; 143-44.
Martin, Rafe – June 23, 2022. Pp. 7-8; 59-61; 111-12; 134-37; 147.
Martin, Winifred Shokai – Sept 30, 2021; Dec 2, 2021. Pp. 52-53; 57-59.
Metcalf, Sally – Jan 14, 2020. Pp. 104-05.
Moore, Meido – Feb 17, 2022. Pp. 14-17; 39; 46-47; 93-94; 114-16; 142-43.
Nelson, Julie – Nov 12, 2019; Feb 25, 2020. Pp. 92-93; 140-41.
Port, Dosho – July 14, 2013; Sept 7, 2014; Oct 31, 2022. Pp. 10; 49; 55;

128-30; 155-56.

Prince-Cherry, Jissai – Sept 16, 2021; Oct 14, 2021. Pp. 106-08; 119.

Pulleyn, John – Nov 15, 2021; Jan 27, 2020. Pp. 23-28; 45; 65-66; 110-11; 121; 147.

Redding, Lila Dené – Sept 14, 2021; Nov 9, 2021. Pp. 147-49; 154-55.

Roitman, Judy – Dec 16, 2021; Feb 10, 2022. Pp. 36-39; 62; 110; 141.

Sheehan, Peggy – July 7, 2022. Pp. 44; 70-72.

Shore, Jeff – Oct 10, 2018. Pp. 53-54; 72-73; 127; 131; 132.

Thornton, Scott – May 29, 2022; Oct 7, 2022. Pp. 28-31; 50-51; 66; 67; 75-76; 130-31; 148.

Weinstein, David – March 10, 2013; May 13, 2013; July 17, 2013; May 19, 2022. Pp. 32-36; 51; 75; 76-80; 134; 152-53.

Glossary

Ango – Ninety day intensive training period.

Awakening – One of several terms referring to achieving experiential insight into the basic interconnectedness of Being.

Blue Cliff Record – See *Hekiganroku*.

Bodhgaya – Village in the Indian state of Bihar considered to be the site of the Buddha's enlightenment.

Bodhicitta – The intention to achieve Awakening for the benefit of others.

Bodhidharma – Legendary Indian figure who brought Zen to China. Bodhidharma is considered the 28th patriarch of Indian Buddhism and the first patriarch of Chinese Zen.

Bodhisattva – An enlightened (Bodhi) being (sattva). Certain historic or legendary Bodhisattvas function much the same as saints in the Christian tradition.

Bompu Zen – Meditation practiced for health benefits.

Buddha – Literally, "The Awakened One." When used with a capital B, usually referring to the historic Buddha, Siddhartha Gautama. With a lower-case b, it refers to any enlightened being.

Buddhadharma – The understanding of reality as taught by the Buddha.

Buddha Hall – In temples, the hall where devotional activities such as chanting are carried out. The hall normally contains an image of the Buddha.

Buddhahood – The state of being fully Awakened.

Buddha Nature – The inherent ability of all sentient (and in some views non-sentient) beings to realize their True Nature.

Budo – Japanese collective term for martial arts.

Chan – Chinese term which the Japanese pronounced as "Zen," meaning meditation.

Chao-chou Ts'ung-shen – cf. Zhaozhou Congshen.

Chi – Energy or source of energy.

Dai- – A prefix meaning "great," as in Dai-kensho.

Daijo Zen – Meditation practices associated with Mahayana Schools other than Zen.

Dhammapada – A collection of the Buddha's teachings rendered into verse. Copies have been found dating back to 500 CE.

Dharma – A term with multiple meanings but generally referring to the teachings of Buddhism.

Dharma Heir – The heir of a Zen teacher whose understanding of the Dharma qualifies them to be a teacher as well.

Dharma Transmission – see Transmission.

-do – A suffix referring to a room or space dedicated to a specific activity or purpose. A zendo, for example, is a space in which Zen (meditation) is practiced.

Dogen Kigen – 13th century Japanese Buddhist credited with bringing Soto Zen to Japan.

Dokusan – Private interview between student and teacher. Cf. Sanzen.

Dukkha – Unsatisfactoriness. Sometimes translated as "suffering."

Eightfold Path – see Four Noble Truths.

Ekayana – Literally the "one vehicle," also rendered as "one path" as in the "one path" to Awakening.

Emptiness – A basic and easily misunderstood Buddhist concept regarding the nature of Reality. Essentially, emptiness refers to an intuition (rather than an intellectual understanding) of the fact that all things are empty of self-nature, i.e., are composed of a variety of elements which are in a constant state of flux and are interdependent with all other elements. The term may also refer to the formless – and yet creative – Void from which all things arise and to which they return.

Enlightenment – Recognition of one's True Nature; experiential insight into the basic interconnectedness of Being.

Four Noble Truths – 1) All of existence is characterized by suffering (dukkha); 2) Suffering is caused by craving; 3) Suffering can be ameliorated by overcoming craving; 4) Craving can be overcome by following the Noble Eightfold path, which consists of right view, right intention, right speech, right action, right livelihood, right effort, right mindfulness, and right meditation.

Four Vows – 1) To save (liberate) all beings; 2) to eliminate endless blind passions; 3) to pass innumerable Dharma Gates; 4) to achieve the great way of Buddha. Cf. Appendix 2.

Gassho – To bring the palms of the hands together often accompanied by a bow. It is a sign of respect and reverence.

Gateless Gateway – see *Mumonkan*.

Gautama – The Buddha's family name. See Siddhartha Gautama.

Gedo Zen – Meditation practice associated with non-Buddhist sects.

Guifeng Zongmi – Tang dynasty Buddhist monk and scholar.

Hakuin Ekaku – 18th century Japanese Zen monk and reformer of the koan tradition.

Hekiganroku – A classic koan collection, also known as the *Blue Cliff Record*.

Householder – Buddhist term for the laity, people who are not monastics.

Ignation Exercises – A series of spiritual exercises – reflections and prayers – composed by Ignatius of Loyola, the founder of the Jesuit Order in the 16th century.

-ji – A suffix meaning "temple."

Joshu Jushin – See Zhaozhou Congshen.

Jukai – Vowing to abide by the Buddhist Precepts. It is the equivalent of formally becoming a Buddhist.

Karma – Literally, "action." The concept in Asian thought that actions have consequences. Popularly viewed as one's past actions, in this or previous lives, resulting in one's current situation.

Karuna – Compassion.

Kensho – Seeing into one's True Nature. Enlightenment.

Koan – (The plural of "koan" is "koan.") Usually an anecdote from the lives of the Zen masters of the past – primarily those in China – often expressed in the form of a question. The question or situation described becomes the focus of a Zen student's meditative practice and helps the student attain insight. While koan cannot be resolved through reasoning, an understanding of them can be achieved through intuition. Individual koan are referred to as "Cases," in the sense of legal precedence in jurisprudence.

Kwan Um – The Korean School of Zen established by Seung Sahn.

Linji – The original Chinese name of Rinzai.

Mahayana – "The Greater Vehicle." The Buddhist tradition which evolved from the earlier Theravada tradition. Zen is a form of Mahayana Buddhism.

Mahamudra – Tibetan Buddhist practice focused on overcoming dualistic perception.

Mantra – A word, phrase, or short prayer which is repeated as a focus of meditation.

Metta – Loving-kindness.

Mu – "Wu" in Chinese. Meaning, "No, not, nothing." Usually refers to the opening koan in the *Mumonkan*: A student of the way asked Joshu, "Does a dog have Buddha Nature?" Joshu replied, "Mu!"

Mumonkan – A classic koan collection, also known as *The Gateless Gate*.

Nonduality – "Not two." The recognition that elements which seem to be distinct are, in fact, not separate but are aspects of a single wholeness.

Oryoki – A formal way of eating using three nested bowls.

Osho – Priest.

Prajna – Wisdom.

Realization – Realization of one's True Nature, and therefore realization of the True Nature of all of Being. Awakening.

Rinzai – The School of Zen practice derived from Linji Yixuan.

Rinzai-ji – "Rinzai Temple," Joshu Sasaki's primary temple located in Los Angeles.

Roshi – Literally, "Old Teacher." In North American Zen, it has come to mean a fully qualified Zen teacher.

Saijojo Zen – Meditation practice undertaken to achieve awakening and integrate it into one's life.

Samadhi – The state of concentration or meditative absorption.

Samsara – The repeated cycle of birth, life, and death.

Samu – Work practice, especially during a sesshin. Carrying out manual tasks needed to maintain the zendo.

Sanbo Zen – Formerly, Sanbo Kyodan. A school of Zen prominent in the West which combines Soto and Rinzai practices. Also known as the Harada/Yasutani Lineage.

Sangha – The community.

Sanzen – Private interview between student and teacher. Cf. Dokusan.

Satori – Awakening, enlightenment.

Sensei – (The plural of "sensei" is "sensei.") Teacher. In American Zen, usually implying less authority than a Roshi would have.

Sesshin – (The plural of "sesshin" is "sesshin.") A Zen retreat, traditionally seven days long.

Shikan Taza – Simple awareness as a meditation practice. In shikan taza, the meditator does not have a particular focus, such as the breath or a koan.

Shojo Zen – Meditation practiced for psychological benefit.

Shoken – Taking individual vows with a single teacher.

Shugyo – Deep body/mind training.

Siddhartha Gautama – The Buddha's given name.

Sodo – A formal training monastery.

Sokoji – Ethnic Buddhist temple in San Francisco to which Shunryu Suzuki was assigned.

Soto – The School of Zen descending from So̱zan Honjaku and To̱zan Ryokai.

Sutra – In Buddhism, scriptural writings usually, but not always, attributed to the Buddha.

Tai Chi Chuan – A Chinese martial art also used as a form of meditation.

Teisho – A formal talk given by a Zen teacher.

GLOSSARY

Theravada – "The Teachings of the Elders." Generally considered an earlier form of Buddhism from which the Mahayana was derived. The form of Buddhism now common in Sri Lanka, Burma and Thailand.

Three Characteristics of Existence – Annica (impermanence), dukkha (suffering), anatta (no permanent self).

Three Gems – see Three Refuges

Three Poisons – Greed, ignorance, and hatred.

Three Refuges – Buddhists take "refuge" in the Buddha, the Dharma, and the Sangha.

Three Treasures – see Three Refuges.

Transmission – Formal recognition that an individual has completed their training and may teach independently.

True Nature – True nature is characterized by nonduality and interdependence with the whole of Being.

Upaya – Skillful means. The variety of techniques used by a teacher to assist a student to come to Awakening.

Vajrayana - Tibetan Buddhism viewed as a third stream of Buddhism alongside the Theravadan (Hinayana) and the Mahayana.

Vinaya - The part of the traditional Buddhist canon which focuses on rules of behavior for monastics. The number of regulations can vary, but in general there are 253 rules governing men and another 95 – for a total of 348 – rules for women.

Vipassana – Meditation techniques associated with Theravada Buddhism.

Zabuton – The mat on which a meditation cushion (zafu) is placed.

Zafu – "Budda" (fu) "seat" (za). A meditation cushion.

Zazen – Seated (za) meditation (zen).

Zen – Literally, "meditation." Zen Buddhism is the meditation school of Buddhism.

Zendo – Room or hall in which Zen is practiced.

Zenji – A teacher of the Dharma.

Zhaozhou Congshen – Ninth century Chan master. His "mu" (cf.) is one of the most commonly assigned initial koans. In the archaic Wade-Giles rendition, Chao-chou Ts'ung-shen. In Japanese, Joshu Jushin.

Author's note

I have used some of the material quoted in this book elsewhere. At times, there are differences in the manner in which those passages are expressed. This is due to changes requested by those to whom they have been attributed.

www.ingramcontent.com/pod-product-compliance
Lightning Source LLC
Chambersburg PA
CBHW030140170426
43199CB00008B/147